FIRSBY

PORTRAIT OF A COUNTRY JUNCTION

FRONTISPIECE Firsby station and level crossing with the threat of closure hanging over it but still smiling in the summer sunshine. Looking much as it always did, but with the signals shorn of their smart finials, and without the tall chimney to the pump house which had been a landmark for quite a distance around. The date is Thursday 30 July 1964, and the train is also something unknown in former times, a parcels train, the 4-36 pm up. Parcels used to travel by any and all passenger trains, but when all local services became two car diesel units with little van space an independant parcels service became necessary.

COVER PHOTOGRAPHS

Front. A view into Firsby Station from the trackside by the signalbox in August 1962, with K3 No. 61956 almost at the end of its days hauling the 6-9 pm up train. An LNER locomotive hauling LNER coaches.

Rear, upper, Firsby South junction and signalbox in August 1964 as train 1E80 for Skegness, the 9-15 am from Nottingham Victoria, negotiates the junction in charge of B1 No. 61390.

Rear, lower, B1 No. 61210 in charge of the 1-23 pm from Skegness to Leicester Central coming under the bridge and past the signalbox at Firsby East in August 1964.

FIRSBY

PORTRAIT OF A COUNTRY JUNCTION

GORDON H BROWN

First published 1994

ISBN 0-9523993-0-X

British Library Cataloguing in Publication Data:
A catalogue record for this book is available from the British Library

Designed and published by the author at Hitchin, Hertfordshire. SG40QE.

Printed by WT Design & Print Ltd., Rough Hill Farm, Loveclough, Rossendale, BB48UG. Tel. 0706 213277.

CONTENTS

For the Railwaymen of Firsby

FOREWORD AND ACKNOWLEDGEMENTS

The idea for this volume arose when retirement allowed time and opportunity to start compiling an album of my photographs of Firsby station and its trains, and in my vanity I imagined that a booklet of some of them might perhaps be of interest to others also. To me, of course, every picture tells a story, and it was suggested that some of the stories should be added as a supporting text to a larger range of photographs. And so we have a stroll down memory lane - or perhaps I should say a steam along memory line! - recalling people and activities into a vignette of a country junction at work. There is a little historical background to set the scene for those readers who know not Firsby, but I must emphasise that this is not a piece of historical research, only memories. Others doubtless will have have different - maybe contradictory - recollections, but all will be right, for practices varied with circumstance and who was on duty. This book then simply puts together my own observations, personal reminiscences and photographs offered by one individual as a tribute to the railway of his native village and to those many people who made the pursuit of his hobby both enjoyable and instructive. To them I am greatly indebted, too many to name them all, though special mention must be made of Mr. Barford (ticket collector), Mr. Elston (pump house attendant), and last but most importantly Mr. Easter (signalman). Thanks are also due to British Railways for providing information in response to my enquiries and for granting facilities, notably for the visit to Firsby Station Box. And I am especially grateful to Mr. Harold Penson, a long serving Firsby railwayman now in his eightyfirst year, and his family for their advice and for checking the script, and to Mrs. Thornley and Mrs. Sharpe for identifying many of the people portrayed. Thanks, too, to my family for their encouragement and help, especially to my two sons: Jonathan my editor and layout adviser, and Philip for setting up the computer programme and correcting my mistakes; to my late parents for presenting me with that first box camera; to my late father-in-law from whose phenominal photographic skill I learnt a lot; and finally to my mother-in-law whose persistance eventually spurred me into thinking that I might just be capable of producing this book.

CHAPTER 1

INTRODUCTION

Firsby, 'junction for Wainfleet, Skegness and Spilsby'. For the whole of my childhood and adolescence my family lived in a cottage about a furlong from Firsby station, close enough for my father to have mastered the art of leaving home to catch the train just as it was drawing into the station, a skill which he practised until the railway closed. It was said that trains have been authorised to depart with remarks such as "Right away, Mr. Brown has arrived!" as Father boarded the train! From my bedroom window I had an unrestricted view across the fields to the lines south of the station going away towards Boston and branching off to Spilsby and Skegness.

Living in this cottage undoubtedly had some bearing on my interest in railways in general and steam engines in particular; that interest I have been told was evident at a very early age. This, I think, is probably true, for some while before I was old enough for school I can clearly remember being 'looked after' by older children and my extreme exasperation when for my amusement they drew trains with red engines and ordinary lower quadrant signals, whereas I knew perfectly well that engines were black or green, and signals were not a bit like the ones they drew. Of course some years afterwards when I could read the *Meccano Magazine* I realised that there actually were some red engines and that there were other sorts of signal too.

Soon I began to haunt the station at every opportunity, delighting in watching the trains, but also observing and noting everything that went on in an attempt to find out all I could. And my reading was to a large extent of railways as well; one of the earliest books I remember being given was called *Puck's Railway Book,* but soon I advanced to more erudite writings and became familiar with such names as O. S. Nock, C. J. Allen, and R. A. H. Weight. In due course I had the satisfaction of daily travel by train, first to school at Spilsby, then to work at Skegness.

In 1935 it was suggested that I might like a camera for Christmas. Realising the possibilities I replied an emphatic "Yes please", and with that rudimentary box Brownie began at Firsby my collection of railway photographs, but not without a little subterfuge on my part! For when the first film was loaded in the camera after Christmas I found myself directed to take photographs of the family, and as the film wound on my anxiety increased with every exposure. Eventually with only two frames left I managed to sneak off to the station without anyone seeing that I had the camera with me. With great delight I exposed those two remaining frames on Atlantic No. 4409 on the up '2 express' (figs 1 & 53). When asked to send the film for development Mother chided "But I thought *we* had a couple left". When the prints arrived she of course had to have the first look, and coming to the last two she exclaimed "I *knew* we had two left" and demanded to know why I had used them at the station. Becoming impatient with adults' apparent lack of understanding I exploded "What on earth did you think I wanted a camera for?", and there followed a stunned silence. But I'll always be grateful that Mother did turn up trumps with the wherewithal for films for me to expose at the station, and that one or two of the results have survived to be included in these pages.

I have used those few early photographs, and others taken after 1945, now with a better camera, together with my memories and written notes, to present a portrait of Firsby as a working country junction from my earliest observations of the 1920s to the end of steam power in 1964, by which time the East Lincolnshire line had been marked for closure. It was a busy place, for a country junction, on some Saturdays in summer busier than many much larger stations. But like all rural stations there were times of great quietude, such as the period from New Year to Easter. In the chapters that follow both the peace and the busy-ness are shown. First we describe the physical layout of the station; then the variety of services calling at or passing through Firsby are discussed in turn - the express passenger trains, the stopping trains, the branch line trains, trains to the seaside, through goods and stopping goods. And finally we see these all fitting together into the working life of this junction. Almost all has gone, swept away by modernisation and rationalisation. True, excursions from Nottingham, Derby, and Burton-on-Trent still traverse the south curve on their way to Skegness, but these are a mere fraction of the traffic that the steam age knew. So the portraits of Firsby presented here - of somersault and upper quadrant signals, the pick-up goods, block signalling, level crossing gates, porters calling out the train's destination - although many are quite recent, come from an age already vanished. And yet, for more than a century those things were the essential characteristics of the country railway.

1 (left) My first railway photograph, frame No 7 of the first spool, New Year 1936. It had to be an Ivatt Atlantic, always one of my favourite classes, and here 4409, a New England engine, is in charge of the 1-45 pm up express to Peterborough, conveying through coaches for Kings Cross. (See also fig 53).

3 (opposite, upper) Another of the earliest of my pictures, probably one from the second film and also in early 1936. An up local train. The engine is either 4358 or 4359, both of which were kept at Wainfleet for a number of years in the 1930s. The station as I remember it, with tall chimney and gas lamps, an interesting comparison with figs 71 & 75 taken from a similar viewpoint. In the bay platform there is a glimpse of the end of the flat-sided ex GNR brake van of the Skegness local train.

4. (opposite, lower) My first 'BR' shot, with BR only just a month old, in February 1948. This is 4537, to give her her old LNER number, one of the regular Spilsby line engines of the LNER period and still carrying out that duty. Many a time in the past it had carried me to and from school. It is in the down sidings with a brake van, having not long before arrived from Spilsby with the daily goods. This must have been one of the first engines to receive BR painting style. When I arrived at the station that afternoon I was greeted by a number of the staff with the exhortation to "come and see our nationalized engine"! and personally conducted to the end of the up platform to take the photograph. In the right foreground is a presentable view of North Box No 6 signal as a disc with LNER lampcase.

2. (above) Almost 30 years have passed since I first pointed the box camera at the GNR Atlantic of fig 1, and for the last time I take this picture of a steam train at Firsby. The time is 7-20 pm on Wednesday 28 July 1965, and the train is the daily summer service from Mablethorpe to Nottingham with 61285 of Colwick in charge. This was the last rostered steam duty on the East Lincolnshire line, and when in the autumn its season of running was over for that year steam working here came to an end.

BRITISH RAILWAYS
E7387

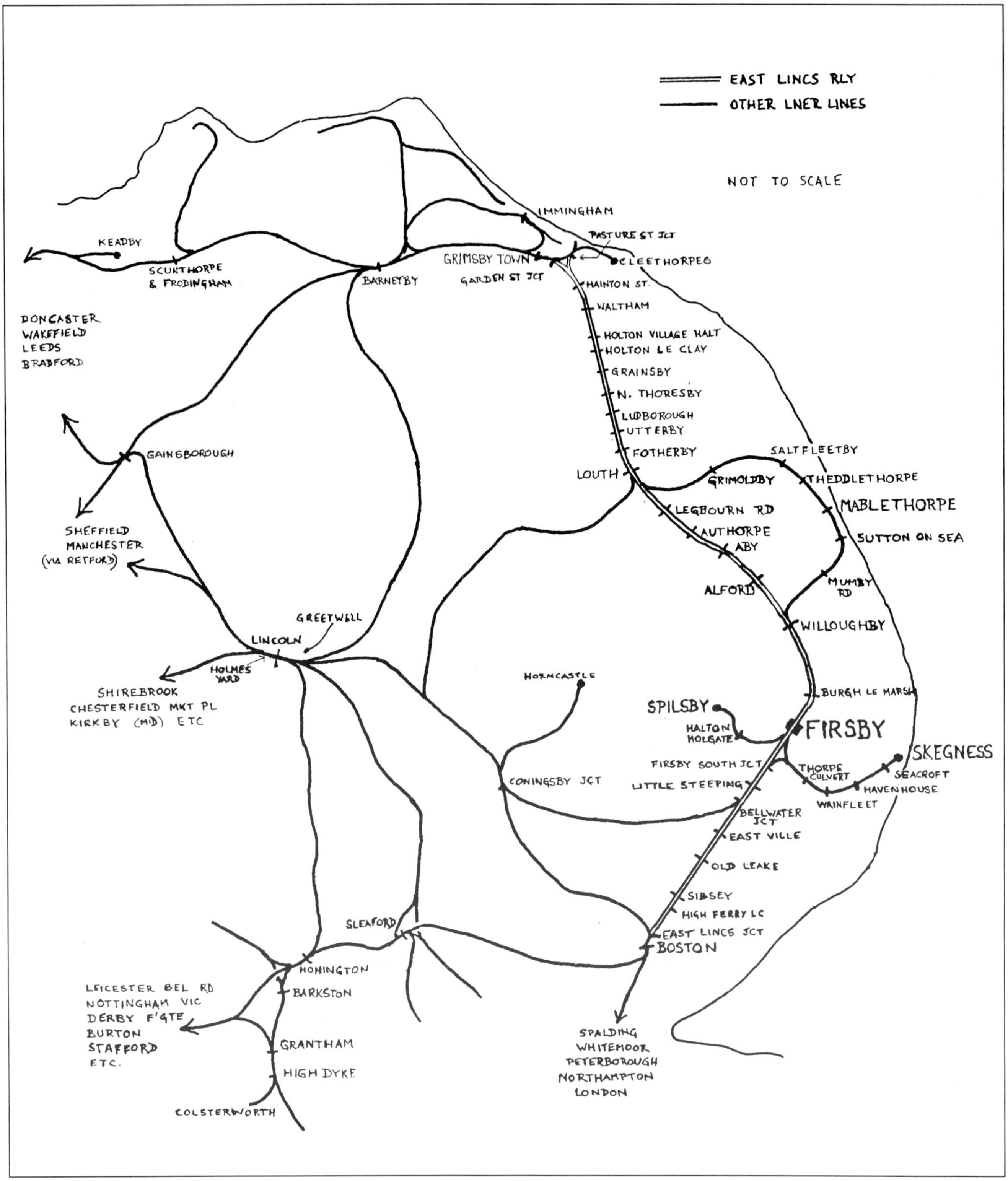

5 The East Lincolnshire Railway and LNER lines in Lincolnshire

CHAPTER 2

THE RAILWAY AT FIRSBY

When the railway arrived at Firsby in 1848 there were some 200 people living in the parish. It was a purely agricultural district. Apart from farmers and farmworkers Firsby had one shopkeeper-cum-beerhouse keeper, one shoemaker, and two corn-millers. Local traffic would therefore be coal and fertilisers inward and farm produce outward, with passengers going to Boston market as an alternative to the road journey to market at Spilsby or Wainfleet.

The railway that came to Firsby was the East Lincolnshire Railway built from a junction with the Manchester, Sheffield & Lincolnshire Railway at Grimsby to link with the Great Northern Peterborough-Lincoln 'loop line' at Boston (fig 5). The Bill for the East Lincolnshire Railway was before Parliament at the same time as the hotly contested Great Northern Railway Bill; the East Lincolnshire Bill, however, was passed apparently with little opposition on 26 June 1846. On 2 December of that year the GNR agreed to lease the ELR, Parliamentary authority being given on 9 July 1847.

It was during 1847-8 that the construction of the railway through Firsby was pushed ahead and the station built. The first of the GNR locomotives to work the line were delivered. Nos 1 & 2, the first of six 'little Sharpies', arrived at Grimsby in August 1847, so we can say for sure that the original GNR No 1 worked through Firsby during 1848-50. Also in

6 The station frontage looking south on 24 May 1970. The main entrance door to the booking hall can be seen under the stone portico. The part of the building shored up was the General Waiting Room, which had been in a poor state for some time. Next to it towards the camera was the Refreshment Room. At the end of the approach drive the entrance gate is standing open, and someone is walking in towards the station. The hedge encloses the garden of the house at the end of the down platform; between the end of this garden and the station building is the 'side entrance' referred to in the text.

1847 another locomotive was delivered to Firsby by road from Lincoln: this engine was most likely another little Sharpie, but might just have been one of the first goods engines, a Hawthorn 0-4-2 or a Bury 0-4-0. Also delivered to the East Lincolnshire in 1847-8 were a dozen passenger coaches and a luggage van, but there were no goods wagons available until the end of 1848. The public train service to Firsby, from Grimsby, commenced on 4 September 1848; the line south to Boston was approved later that month, but the start of service had to await the completion of a temporary GNR platform at Boston in October.

The East Lincolnshire Railway from Grimsby to Boston was built on a course running to the east of the Lincolnshire Wolds across the flat land known as the marsh. On its way south it served Louth, the principal market town for north-east Lindsey, Alford, a smaller town, and Burgh le Marsh, a large village having a small market, before reaching Firsby. Firsby was small by comparison, but its station was evidently intended to serve a wide area, for instead of being located close by the village (as it could easily have been) it was half a mile to the north, where the railway crossed the road from Spilsby to Wainfleet. Here, the station could serve the needs of Irby, Thorpe Culvert and Wainfleet to the east, and Great Steeping and quite likely Spilsby to the west. Firsby must have been regarded by the ELR as of some significance, being provided with an overall roof (which it alone of the stations on this line retained right to the end), an imposing stone portico, and its own gasworks and gas lighting. Such provision seems quite appropriate and indeed advantageous for the junction which Firsby became, but perhaps of doubtful justification for a village passing station. Foresight on the part of the ELR directors, or simply fortuitous? In fact Firsby continued the quiet life of a village station for twenty years. There was a minor accident to a locomotive in 1849, and, probably more spectacular, a gale in 1860 which blew down the original goods shed, so the one that remains is its replacement.

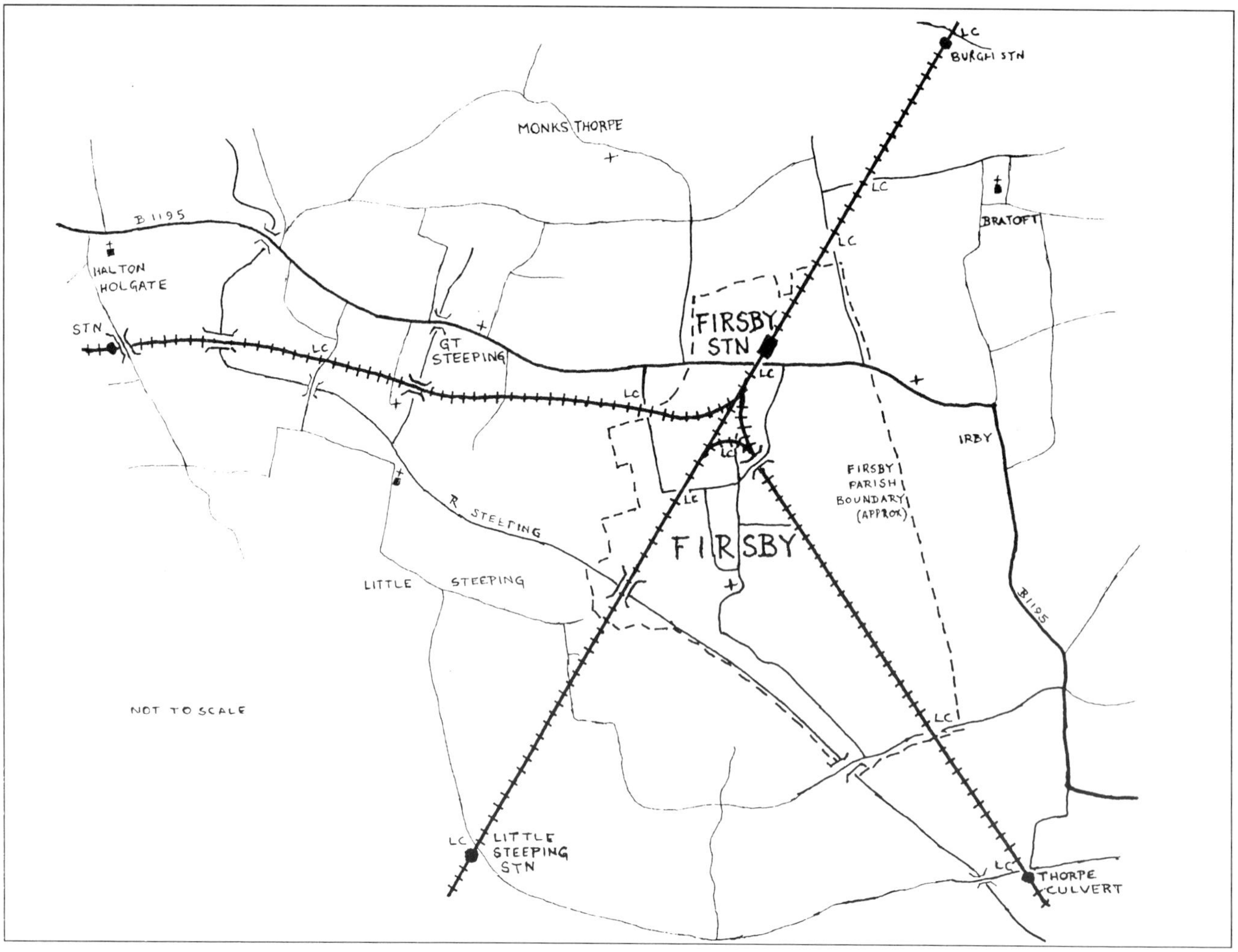

7 Firsby Station and locality

Of course the advantages of a railway in the mid-nineteenth century were not lost upon the people of Spilsby, and after forming a local company, the branch was opened on 1 May 1868. So Firsby became a junction, and acquired a new signalbox commensurate with its new status. The GNR worked the Spilsby line from the start, and about a couple of decades later purchased it, completion taking effect on 1 January 1891. Probably some of the little Sharpies, rebuilt by then, were used on the Spilsby trains.

But before the Spilsby line was open, the folk of Wainfleet had taken a leaf out of Spilsby's book. In those days Wainfleet, like Spilsby, was a market town of some importance. Larger than Skegness, Wainfleet was accessible to small sea-going craft, and so the Wainfleet & Firsby Railway Company was set up to build a line to join the East Lincolnshire. The branch was opened in the Autumn of 1871, and while it was being built the extension to Skegness was promoted as a separate local company, and brought into service on 28 July 1873. Like the Spilsby, the Wainfleet and Skegness line was worked by the GNR from the beginning, and probably more of the rebuilt little Sharpies trotted up and down this line too. As built, the Skegness branch was single track only, and made a simple junction with the up line at Firsby, more or less opposite the Spilsby line junction. It was not long, though, before the bay platform and the layout that I knew came into being.

So, as the well remembered platform name-boards proclaimed, Firsby was now 'junction for Wainfleet, Skegness and Spilsby'. The opening of the Skegness line gave an impetus to the holiday traffic, and almost immediately the GNR sought powers to build Firsby south curve, but it was not brought into use until 1881, in time for the summer traffic of that year. Notwithstanding the single track of the Skegness branch, the curve was double, and brought with it two more signal boxes to Firsby, - the South and the East. That single line to Skegness was soon found to be a handicap for the holiday traffic, and the

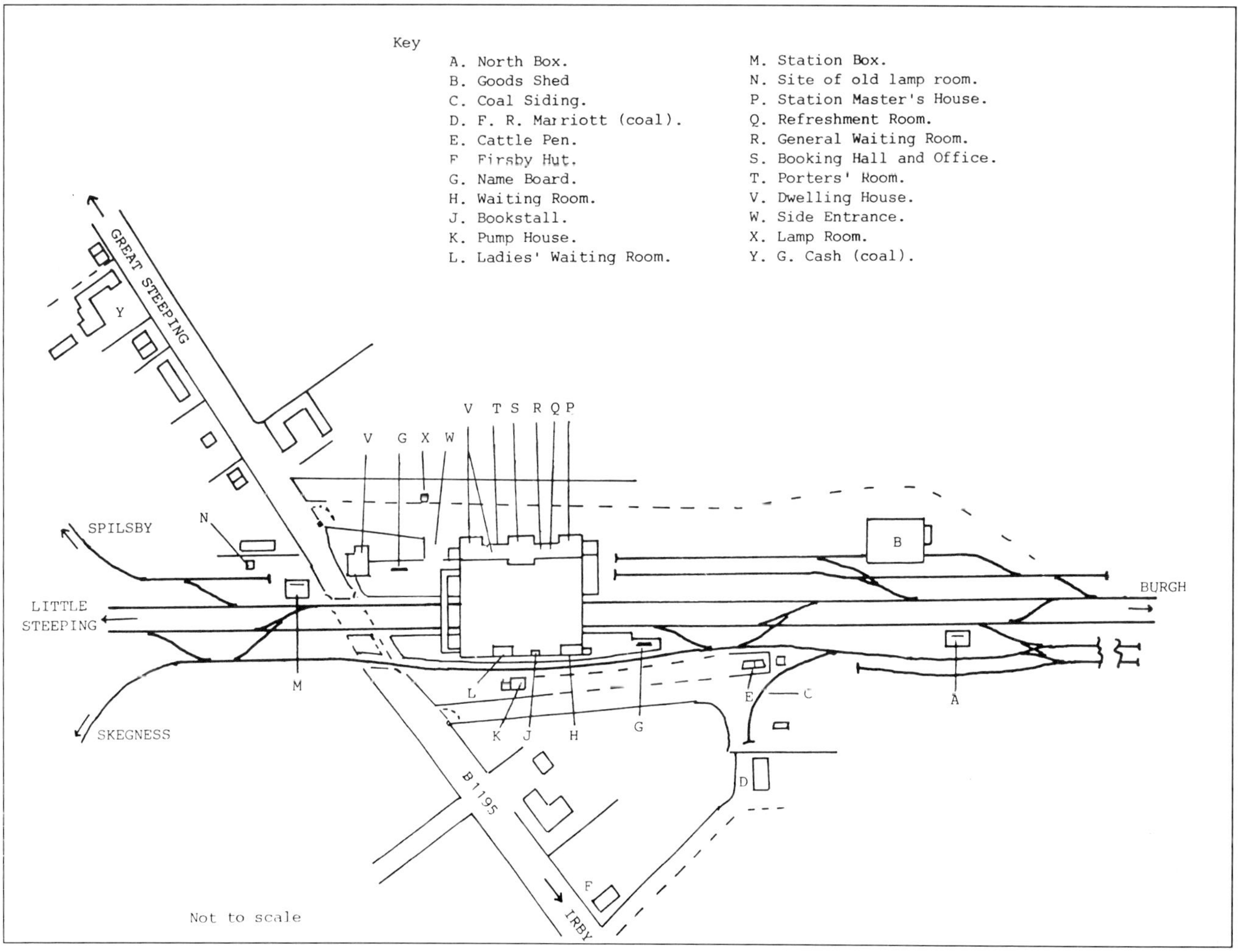

8 Firsby Station area layout showing some features mentioned in the text

9 Firsby station frontage looking north on 16 September 1964 (the occasion of a visit to attend the first of the closure inquiries), with a view along the approach road to the goods shed, seen in the distance. The combination of a basically Georgian-styled building with a stone entrance in renaissance style, on an E shaped layout was not displeasing. The two wings were both dwelling houses. The northern one was occupied by the Station Master: his front door opened on to the down platform. The southern one, nearest the camera, comprised two houses, both the homes of members of the station staff.

GNR were anxious for it to be doubled, but one can well imagine that the local companies would find the capital hard to raise. Eventually the GNR purchased the branch, the transfer taking effect on New Years Day 1896, and without delay plans were drawn up for the doubling, which was completed throughout in the summer of 1900.

And so the final layout of Firsby, shown in fig 138, came into being. There were, though, two further events which affected operations here. The first was the opening in 1913 of the new line between Bellwater Junction and Coningsby, providing a shorter and more direct route from Lincoln. Apart from its value for excursion trains, its opening saw the commencement of the through trains between Skegness and Lincoln (and sometimes Retford and Sheffield) as the daily service along that line, and which called, and reversed, at Firsby. The second was the conversion in 1927 of the points at the East to electric working, and transference of control to the Station Box, of which more in the next chapter.

To end this chapter come with me for a stroll round the station one day in the 1930s (fig 8). Coming along the road from our house we see on the right the end of the signal box projecting beyond the houses, but the gates are half hidden for the railway is below the road which dips down to cross the line. We turn left into the station approach and walk alongside the garden of the railway house at the end of the down platform. On our left is the corrugated iron lamp room, which replaced an earlier one located at the lineside by the Spilsby line safety neck. That earlier one was built of old sleepers and made a spectacular exit with a tall column of black smoke! At the end of the garden to our right is the 'side' entrance to the down platform, but we carry on alongside the station building (fig 9). The end nearest is a house occupied by the station foreman, Mr. Jack Chapman, and his daughter Annie, a porter. Next in a second house lived Mr. Arthur Elston, the pump house attendant.

10 At the North on 18 August 1960, as 64284 of Immingham passes by the Box with a down through goods. The north aspect of the goods shed, and view through shown here, give an idea of the length of the shed, enabling 4 or 5 4-wheelers to be dealt with under cover. Over the door is a notice informimg Engines that they Must Not Pass This Board. A separate crossover and through road south of the goods shed provided direct access to the extended down sidings.

When he moved to a new council house Mr. Doe, a goods checker, took over. (Then in 1939 another station foreman, Mr. Ron Thornley, came to live there.) In the centre of the frontage the imposing stone portico shelters the arched doorway to the booking hall. Continuing towards the yard we pass at the end of the building a small garden with its garden gate. This is the Station Master's garden: the north wing of the building is his house. His front door opens direct on to the extreme end of the down platform, and bears a cast iron notice RESIDENCE, similar in style to the ones lettered FIRSBY and let into the top rails of the platform seats.

As we approach the goods shed we see in the near down siding wagons of coal for Mr. Cash; the yard crane; and various wagons on the inner siding awaiting collection by the pick-up goods. The goods shed is quite a large building with arched windows. A railway Scammel road trailer is being loaded at the shed with various consignments for delivery. Skirting round the north end of the shed we find the old stable which once housed the resident horse. Looking across the tracks we see on the opposite side the North Box (fig 10) which controls the Yard; on that side of the line, too, the coal siding for Mr. Marriott branches off the loop behind the North Box.

Retracing our steps, we enter the station under the impressive portico through the door seen in fig 6, and into the L shaped booking hall. Opposite is the 'office' door to the booking office: here parcels are dealt with. We turn left, then right, along the L of the booking hall: to our left is the door to the general waiting room, on our right the ticket issuing window, ahead the arch leading to the down platform. We notice on the wall of the booking hall an extensive display of handbills with details of all sorts of excursions and services on offer and an invitation to 'please take one'. Prominent among the excursions are the trips to London sponsored by Easons, the Grimsby travel agents. On the platform we hear to our left the rattle of crockery coming from the refreshment room, privately run by Miss Allen, and located between the waiting room and the Station Master's house. It was well equipped, its tea and coffee machine and washing up water heated from the station gas supply. For a time in GNR days my mother worked there; she told me of the brisk business done then, and the crowds using the

11 A view from the station on 8 August 1962 showing the down sidings and goods shed. The large area of the goods shed reflects the business dealt with and the intended catchment area of Firsby. It replaced the one blown down not many years after the line opened. At the platform is the 8-13 am down train.

Wednesday Boston market train and the Spilsby line on Mondays (Spilsby market day). Also, before her marriage, Mrs. Penson worked there in the late 1930s - her husband appears in figs 115 & 129. One of her jobs was to wander along the platform while trains were waiting, selling chocolate etc. from a shoulder-hung tray.

Between the tracks we note the line of cast iron columns and decorated arch sections supporting the slender iron framework of the overall roof, the valence of which is of dentil edged boards (figs 12, 13, 14). The centre columns meant that the platforms were unobstructed, a great advantage on busy summer days. Under the roof the platform surfaces are stone flags, the exposed extensions are blue brick. Along the platform we pass on the right the porters' room and cross to the up platform by the handsome lattice iron footbridge. From the bridge we have a closer look at the roof construction: the rafters and purlins are probably wrought iron. Looking the other way from the bridge there is a good view of the level crossing and signal box, with the Spilsby line curving away to the right, the Skegness to the left, and in the distance the South Box at the end of the curve (fig 16). Along the up platform we note that there is just the long wall supporting the roof; archways give access to the bay platform. On the up platform there are two waiting rooms built of glazed wood panelling, one near the footbridge steps for ladies, and the other general waiting room right at the north end (fig 15). Half way along the platform is the folding lock-up bookstall, in charge of a 'paper boy' from the W. H. Smith bookstall at Boston station. He arrived each day on the 8-30 am down train, along with his supply of newspapers, and spent the next hour or so on a local delivery round, returning to open his bookstall in time for the morning express. The rest of the day he remained on the station, and as well as selling from his bookstall, he would patrol waiting trains with a wicker tray of papers and magazines. The outbreak of war in 1939 put an end to this; as a wartime expedient my mother took on the daily local paper round, and was still doing it in the 1950s.

Arriving at the north end of the platform and looking northwards we see the large cattle pen alongside the extension of the bay platform line (fig 18). Beside us is one of the two large nameboards (fig 17) proclaiming Firsby's junction status. There is a similar one at the other end of the down platform. Quite magnificent structures, built of substantial timber surrounded by a mitred framework of heavy moulding, their message is conveyed by cast metal letters screwed on. In the late 1930s parodies of these appeared high up on the wall under the roof on each side of the station, announcing Firsby to be 'junction for Skegness and Butlin's Holiday Camp'.

Retracing our steps along the blue brick Skegness bay platform: it is completely open, for it is not part of the 1848 design, but was added a few

12 Firsby station from the north, with LNER 2910 of Lincoln on the New Line goods, its driver and fireman posing for the camera while the tender tank fills with water. Taken in 1947. The excellent somersault signal will be noted, - its lattice post complete with finial; and on the left is a glimpse of the large name-board.

13 The northward view of the station in 1962. Some of the boards at the gable ends of the roof have been removed; the pump house chimney has gone; the gas lanterns have been replaced by electric fittings; a modern-day sign hangs beneath the footbridge. This picture gives a good impression of the line of cast iron columns supporting the roof. Firsby was the only ELR station to retain its overall roof to the end. The date is Wednesday 8 August, and the train is an Inspectors' special in charge of a Lincoln engine.

14 A view from the interior of the station from the down platform on Wednesday 31 July 1963, showing detail of the roof supports and ironwork, and the dentil-edged boards. Most of the footbridge is shown too, and the form of its construction is evident: the support columns and stairway balustrades cast iron, while the lattice span is probably wrought iron. The span floor is of wooden boards. Entering the down line from the Skegness line at about 11-30 am is Austerity 90618 hauling empty stock. An empty pigeon basket awaits return to its owner: the release of homing pigeons was a fairly frequent occurrence at Firsby. Partly obscured by the roof support column at the left Mr. Ron Thornley pauses in his task of repainting the white line along the platform edge.

years after the Skegness line had been opened. Half way along, on the opposite side of the bay platform track is the pump house, its tall chimney lazily issuing smoke (fig 15). The entrance door in the wall facing the level crossing opens into the boiler room, which contains a vertical boiler supplying steam at 90 lb to the engines in the next room. The flue passes through the wall and into the base of the chimney. Opposite the entrance door is the arch into the engine room. Here is a pair of 'miniature' beam engines, their beams about eight feet long and about four feet above floor level. Each cylinder is at the near end of the beam, the 'idle' pivot at the far end. A little way along from the cylinder end is the connecting rod, driving the shaft supported on bracket bearings at ground level. The shaft passes through the partition wall to the right into the pump room, where there is a three plunger force pump set deep into the well and driven by 120 degree cranks on the engine shaft.

Continuing along the platform towards the level crossing with its unusual double set of gates (chap 3), we note the cast iron lamp standard with its square gas lantern; a similar one is by the pedestrian handgate by the Skegness line, and a third on the down platform. Crossing the line on the level we return to the down platform, along past the second of the excellent nameboards we arrive at the 'side' entrance, used for mail, newspapers and so on: the alcove formed by the fence and wall being just right for parking the mail van. We may leave by this way - as in practice did most passengers from this side of the station - to retrace our steps along to the road and home.

15 A view into the station from the signal box balcony in 1936, showing the two glazed wooden-panelled waiting rooms on the up platform; also the gas lamp on the footbridge, and a further one peeping up behind the water crane. The tall chimney to the pump house is issuing smoke; the entrance to that building is below its left hand window in the picture. Of note, too, are the elegant finials to the signal posts, removed in later years (chapter 3); and the all-wooden access gate to the signal box, replaced subsequently by one similar to the pedestrian handgate opposite. The train is the 3-45 pm arrival from Spilsby in charge of its regular engine No. 4537, with Driver Barwick watching me take this photograph of him! Beyond the station on the down line is the pick-up goods shown in fig 73.

16 The view to the south from the footbridge as the 6-9 pm train leaves for Boston on Friday 3 August 1962 with K3 No. 61956 in charge, while, after loading parcels and mail, Mr. Albert Skinner trundles an empty barrow towards the crossing, followed by the postman with the postal barrow. Comparing this with figs 15 & 119, there are no finials on the signal posts, there are electric wires strung to the lamp standard and the signal box gable, and the signs are sheet metal instead of cast iron, and bear different wording.

17 (Facing upper) Looking northwards from the down platform as a right-hand drive K3 dashes along with an up fish train at 7 o'clock on a summer evening in 1947. This picture shows one of the handsome large name-boards proclaiming Firsby's status as a junction. They were substantially made, and had screwed on cast metal letters. Hidden during the war, they were quickly restored when peace returned, even though the Spilsby service was still 'suspended'. They were replaced in the 1950s by much less attractive signs bearing the simple legend 'FIRSBY'. Also of note is the substantial wooden planking protecting the rodding to the bolt locks at the North. This made a convenient catwalk between the station and the North Box and goods shed; it was removed in later years, see fig 59. Interesting, too, are the signals: the somersault down inner home (No. 17) with its fine lattice post and finial intact, and the up home by the rear of the train also still a somersault, as was the up distant. By 1957 No. 17 was upper quadrant, and had lost its finial, the others following in the early 1960s.

18 (Facing lower) The up side of the yard viewed from the up platform on 17 August 1960. On the right the cattle pen is clearly seen, and in the distance is the North Box, with the signalman just visible. Engine 61766 has just attached a van to the rear of an up train, the shunter, Mr. Carey, stands by as the engine is about to return to the sidings, for which North Box No 6 disc can be seen at clear.

FIRSBY
WAINFLEET
SKEGNESS & SPILSBY

61766

19 (Left) A view into the South Box, showing, through the windows, the signalman at the desk making up the train register as 61382 heads the 11-17 from Skegness to Leeds via the New Line and the joint line to Doncaster on Saturday 3 August 1963.

21 (opposite, below) The South Box looking south on Saturday 1 August 1964. The lever frame and block shelf are visible through the window, and through the doorway can be seen levers 11, 12, 13, and 5 pulled off to set the road for the passing train, its progress watched by the signalman standing at the far end of the Box. The differing angles at which the levers lean when pulled off are apparent, for some levers had a greater throw than others, presumably to provide extra purchase for difficult ones. The train is 1E93, the 8-30 from Kings Norton, travelling by way of Burton-on-Trent, Derby Friargate and the GNR route through Netherfield and Boston; the engine is 61141.

20 (Left) The South Box looking north on Saturday 3 August 1963, with 61092 in charge of the 3-17 pm from Skegness to Derby Friargate. The tail of the train can be seen to the right of the picture as it follows round the curve.

CHAPTER 3

SIGNALS AND SIGNALBOXES

An indication of the relative importance of Firsby might be gained from its possession of four signalboxes, something one might expect of a large main line station perhaps, rather than at a country station the size of Firsby. The need for this number was occasioned by the extent of the triangle junctions and yard layout, and served as a reminder of the often relatively complex operations which took place. A complete 1930s signalling diagram appears at the end of this book as a fold-out page (fig 138): as well as illustrating this chapter it will be found helpful in following the sequences of chapter 9 where the operation of the signalling is referred to in some detail.

The three signalboxes at the corners of the triangle controlled the running lines and the traffic. Of these the Station was the most important, certainly the busiest, and was a Special Class box, though the South had its moments of glory on summer Saturdays and Bank Holidays. Block sections from the adjacent stations - Burgh, Thorpe Culvert, and Little Steeping (fig 7) - terminated at the Station, East, and South boxes respectively. Further block circuits linked the three boxes to control the triangle itself. The single line Spilsby branch was worked 'one engine in steam' with a simple train staff which was the key to the siding points at Halton and Spilsby. A single wire omnibus telephone circuit provided communication between Firsby, Halton, Spilsby, and the busier level crossings on the branch. In the early 1930s the permanent way gang was provided with a petrol

trolley and so the old train staff was replaced by a more complex electric staff system, the staff still the key to the points, with end-to-end interlocking taking place via the wire of the telephone circuit. In addition to the train staff carried on the engine there was an 'occupation token' for the trolley. This was normally locked in a socket which was fitted on the block shelf in the Station Box. In Spilsby booking office there were sockets for the token and the staff. Thus when the train was safely at Spilsby the token could be released for the trolley to travel over the branch, locking the staff until the trolley token was replaced in its socket at either Firsby or Spilsby. One of the signalmen commented that a socket for the staff at Firsby could have avoided delay to permanent way work, for the train often stayed at Firsby long enough for the trolley to traverse the length of the branch. A further safety measure was the electric lock fitted at Firsby to the Spilsby line starting signal, No. 23. When ready to depart, the engine driver released this lock by means of the train staff, which allowed one pull only of the signal; its use is mentioned in chapter 9.

The Station signalbox was the one built new for the opening of the Spilsby line in 1868. The South and East were provided in 1881 when the curve came into use; both contained a 20 lever Saxby & Farmer rocker frame. The South was manned by a visiting relief signalman during the summer holiday season. At all other times, except for special movements round the curve, it was switched out with all its main line signals pulled off and the Little Steeping block circuit switched through to the Station Box. The East, though, once the Skegness line had been doubled, had to be manned throughout the year because of the

22 Firsby Station Box in 1963 as most people saw it, - from the public crossing. The finish of the name-board should be noted - black lettering on a light ground, a complete reversal of pre-nationalization practice (fig 73). The name-boards are wide boards with a substantial surround and additional moulding inside the main surround. The letters are cast metal, screwed on. Presumably the revised finish was easier to apply - the light background (the same colour as the gable end?) being applied all over with gay abandon, and the black overlaid subsequently, a method not easy with white letters on a black ground! The train is ironstone for Frodingham hauled by Gresley 2-8-0 No. 63984.

23 Firsby Station Box in 1963 seen from the bank alongside the Skegness line, as a parcels train passes. Clearly apparent is the '4-bay' construction, each bay having a window to the interlocking floor. As built for the opening of the Spilsby line the Box had three bays only, - I can clearly remember the extra bay being built on, at the end remote from the camera in the picture, in 1927, to accommodate the longer lever frame necessary when control of the East junction was transferred that year. Comparison with fig 38 shows that the upper part of the chmney stack has been rebuilt : this occurred between the summers of 1957 & 1960.

24 Firsby East Signal Box, at 7-45 pm on Wednesday 29 July 1964. The'spring points' notice refers to the junction points on the down line, which, after 1927, were spring controlled and biassed to be set for the line from the station. This was perfectly in order because to all passenger trains these points are always trailing, and are pushed over by the wheel flanges of trains coming round the curve from the South and which are always travelling at a low speed. The East Box ceased to be a signal box in 1927, and since then has housed banks of primary batteries to provide power for the point motors and track circuits. The train is the 7-26 from Skegness to Derby Friargate in charge of Colwick engine 61210. Overshadowing the Box is the East road bridge, built to overcome the difficulties caused by there being two level crossings within 100 yards of each other after the south curve was built. See captions to figs 79, 91, and 99.

double-to-single line transition between there and the station. However, in 1927 the points at the East were converted to electric operation, and control of that junction transferred to the Station Box. I can clearly remember the extra 'bay' being built on to the end of the Station Box nearest to the level crossing to make room for a longer lever frame. The installation of the new 56 lever frame had to take place while the box was still working, which is why after the changeover the Station signalman worked the frame with his back to the running lines, the opposite of normal practice. The East box became a battery house, for in those days there was neither mains electricity nor prospect of such, and all the equipment had to be operated from 'wet' leclanche cells, quite an achievement then. The two electrically operated sets of points at the East (levers No. 8 & 7), usually referred to as 'the motors', were always worked together, it being arranged that both were reversed to bring a train from the Skegness line into the station, and both normal for all other movements. Closure of the East Box and bringing all of the one arm of the triangle under control of the Station Box meant that the Thorpe Culvert block circuit now terminated in the Station Box, though the block section itself still ended at the East junction.

About a dozen track circuits were provided, covering the single line, the down line of the curve, the East and Skegness line towards Thorpe, and a couple on the down main line at the Station and North. An 'illuminated' track diagram was provided in the Station Box, of polished oak, 5 ft x 2 ft 6 in x 7 in. The 'backing' for the diagram was made up of vertical boards with apertures through which the indicators show. The diagram was fronted by quarter-inch plate glass. Originally the track circuit indicators were dolls eyes, and J track, which was not provided until 1937-8, had no dolls eye. It appears that the signalmen were told that they did not need a dolls eye to see a train under their noses, but I pointed out that the dolls eye was also a fault indicator, and without it the first sign of trouble would be the unexplained locking up of levers. The original diagram had a comprehensive table of locking derived from the track circuits; this did not appear on the later diagram provided after the complete closure of the Spilsby line, and which appears in the pictures, see fig 26. This final diagram used lamps as track circuit indicators. The original vertical boards were moved around in the oak frame to enable the apertures for the lamp fittings to be cut, and it appears that a change of heart had taken place for J track has a lamp!

During LNER days the Station Box was manned in 2 full and one half shift. The two full time signalmen, Messrs Easter and Stones, alternated on early and late shifts. The half shift in the middle of the day was covered by Mr. Roberts. He also manned the South for the occasional special movements round the curve out of season.

25 A rear view of Firsby North Box in the evening of Saturday 4 August 1962, as the 7 pm express from Kings Cross to Cleethorpes departs in charge of 70038 *Robin Hood.*

26 Inside Firsby Station Box on Tuesday 4 August 1964, looking towards the station. The picture shows the illuminated track diagram referred to in the text. A train has left the down platform for Skegness, as witness the through road set (28, 29, 32, 33), and track D occupied on the diagram. The duty signalman, Mr. Moore, is waiting for the train to clear No 28 locking bar so that he can restore the points. Meantime the summer relief signalman is opening the gates.

The fourth signalbox at Firsby was the 25-lever North Box, which controlled the goods yard, and which to me seemed unusual and a particular indicator of Firsby's status. Was it, I wonder, the original Firsby signal box, relegated when the arrival of the Spilsby line necessitated a new signal box by the level crossing? The North Box was not a block post; the various sections of its lever frame were released by four 'bolt locks' actuated by levers in the Station Box. In November 1958 these mechanical locks were replaced by electric locks, still under the control of the same four levers in the Station Box. There was a direct telephone circuit between the North and Station Boxes, and also a separate signalling bell circuit, coded rings on the latter being used to co-ordinate the operation of the bolt locks, and for other traffic control requirements. The North was manned as required by the yard work and must have been a valuable asset when the yard was busy in the hey-day of goods traffic before road competition began to take its toll.

As already mentioned, among my early memories of Firsby was the extensive array of somersault signals - a hall-mark of the GNR in its later decades (see bibliography). As well as the usual square wooden signal posts the GNR used slender and quite handsome lattice posts and brackets, each crowned by a ball and spike finial (figs 12, 15, 18). Later, concrete posts, with squat square finials, came into use (figs 32 & 33), and also fluted metal arms instead of timber (fig 29). All these variations resulted in some interesting signals, and Firsby had an excellent collection, as the pictures illustrate. A feature of the somersault was that without special fittings the arm could be set at the top of the post for daylight viewing, and the spectacle mounted separately lower down the post for better visibility at night. I remember at least four in this form at Firsby: the South down distant; the Spilsby line home signal (No. 19); and two at the East, the single line down home No. 13, and the down starter No. 12. Of these four it was the Spilsby line signal which became the first to be changed to an upper quadrant, this took place in the early 1930s.

27 Firsby North Signal Box in the sun as 92038 charges past with an up fish train at about 6-10 pm on Wednesday 31 August 1963. The shunter's pole will be seen, propped against the handrail of the steps; kept there handy for use when a pick up goods arrived. It appears, too, in a number of other pictures which include this aspect of the North Box. Again, comparing this picture with fig 58 illustrates the revised finish to the name-board.

The ball and spike finials were removed in early BR days, on the instructions of 'Higher Authority' I was told. The wooden ones went first. The lattice ones presented a problem: the finials were integral with the posts and not easily detached! Indeed, I was given to understand that it was only the insistance of a representative of 'Higher Authority' that caused their eventual removal - with some difficulty and a hacksaw. Why these signals should have been disfigured in this way is difficult to understand, for signals elsewhere remained undamaged for many years thereafter.

After grouping upper quadrants appeared. The first one at Firsby was the South up main home, in the 1920s. Then followed the Spilsby line home signal (No. 19), and the down main starter (No. 18). Towards the end of the LNER and in BR days more upper quadrants appeared until by the final years only the multiple arm signals and a couple of single ones remained somersaults.

28 One of the few single somersault signals that remained at Firsby to the end, the South up 'branch' home: wooden post and wooden arm. It is here seen from the rear as 43158 comes round from Skegness with a return goods on Wednesday 31 July 1963. A front view of this signal appears in fig 95.

29 At the other end of the curve is the East junction up home signal, an assembly of concrete sections held together by nuts and bolts, and having arms of ribbed metal. The arm at clear is Station Box No. 5 signalling a train from Skegness into the station. The other home arm is Station Box No. 2, controlling trains round to the South; beneath it is the South Box up 'branch' distant, South lever No. 20. The white sign vaguely resemblimg a D, which is attached to the main post, directs the enginemen, if brought to a stand at this signal, to call the box by means of the telephone provided in the cabinet marked with diagonal black and white stripes.

30 The sun shines on the South down home signal on Saturday 31 August 1963. Still attractive although the finials have been removed. One of the GNR all-lattice structures at Firsby, equipped with timber arms. The pair of arms to the left apply to the main line: the home (upper) is South Box lever No. 2, beneath it is the Station Box down distant (No. 15). The arms to the right apply to the curve to the East junction for Skegness trains: the upper (home) is South Box lever No. 5, the arm beneath it is the East down distant, Station Box lever No. 10.

31 Looking up at the South down home signal, showing some details of the mechanism, with the home signal at clear for a down train to the station. The three slots to the main line distant will be noticed. The first slot, with the weight down in the normal position, is the one for the distant itself, Station Box lever No. 15. The rearmost slot with the smaller weight closer to the pivot is the home arm which is pulled off, South Box lever No. 2. The third slot is activated by South Box lever No. 3, its down main starter, which is itself a slot on the Station down main home: that signal thus serves a dual purpose. (So does the South up main home: it doubles as the Station up starter.) This third slot, too, is clear, the train having been accepted by the Station and so the South has pulled off all his down main signals. The distant arm is held on by its own slot, Station Box lever No. 15, presumably until the Station has obtained clear from Burgh and closed the gates. It will be noted that the East distant (on the right) has but two slots as the South has no 'branch' (Skegness curve) starter.

32 & 33 What used to be the three-arm signal on the down platform, photographed in May 1970. The lowest of the three arms controlled the route to the Spilsby line: it was replaced by the disc shown in the pictures following the complete closure of the Spilsby line. It is lever No. 23. The top arm, No. 34, shown at clear in Fig 32, controls trains leaving the down platform for Skegness. The second arm, No. 37, controls trains leaving the down platform for Little Steeping and thence Boston or Lincoln. It is seen at clear in fig 33, and in this view too the fixing holes for the third arm originally fitted can be seen. In fig 32 Mr. P. Lord, the signalman, is standing in the Box doorway. This signal in its original form appears in figs 51 and 73. Though labelled on the lever frame as "miniature", it was a running signal, and in the nineteenth century it was a full size 3-post bracket junction structure of timber construction located at the foot of the platform end ramp. Its replacement by this signal was occasioned by road widening in the twentieth century.

34 & 35 The up main inner home signal, lever No. 38. This signal had a 'travelling' access ladder, doubtless provided when it was moved nearer to the platform end for the road widening mentioned on the previous page. The ladder foot was supported by a roller that moved over the crossing timbers, while the top of the ladder was fixed by short bars pivoted between itself and a bracket on the post. When extended the hinged metal strut near the bottom of the ladder was engaged in a stirrup on the post. The ladder was folded back when not in use to avoid obstructing the public crossing.

36 & 37 The starting signal for the bay platform line. The upper arm, No. 14, reads from the platform to the Skegness line: it is shown in Fig 36 (left) at clear for a local train about to leave. The lower arm, No. 36, reads from the bay platform to the up main line. Fig 37 (right) shows it at clear for a train to cross to the up main line on its way to Bellwater Junction and Lincoln.

38 & 39 Various items of electrical equipment formed an essential part of the signalling system, and here we have two illustrations of linemen at work maintaining the overhead wires linking the signal boxes with each other and with the electrical devices at the lineside. In fig 38, left, taken in 1936-7, a lineman, believed to be Mr. Wilf Barton, is working on the pole by the chimney corner of the Station Box. The large number of wires leading into the Box was necessary for the control of the East junction. Taken ten years later, fig 39, right, shows Mr. Clayton (uppermost) clearing a fault at the pole by the goods shed. Assisting him at the pole top is Mr. Dunk; the third member of the working party, Mr. Joe Blakey, was assisting from the ground but climbed the pole at my request to be included in the picture. Other S & T men were Messrs John Thornley and Jack Geary; and in LNER days John Would and Ben Knight (whose daughter Daisy eventually took over the booking office).

40 As part of the block telegraph, lineside repeater indicators were provided to warn of the approach of trains. Shown here are the indicators at No. 57 crossing near Firsby South. The right hand indicator, for the up line, is deflected to the left, indicating TRAIN IN SECTION for a train travelling towards Little Steeping.

41 Not often was an Ivatt Atlantic seen hauling a passenger train tender first! This one was on a through train for Skegness, probably from Grantham or Nottingham, and which called at the station. This box camera shot was almost certainly taken in 1938. At the right of the picture is one of the original GNR type shunting discs. This one is Station Box lever No. 9: it controlled the movement of engines setting back from the down Skegness line to the station as part of the process of turning on the triangle. It appears in its final form in fig 120.

42 Another 1930s photograph, with class J2 No. 3072 at the down platform. In the right foreground is disc No. 41, a GNR rotating disc mechanism with LNER square lamp case and aspect plate. See also fig 43.

All the shunt signals at Firsby were originally the standard GNR rotating ground discs. They had open heads made of two discs spaced apart by a curved plate and threaded rods. The lamp insert had glasses in two adjacent sides, one shone through the red bull in the front red disc, the other through the open side for 'clear' (fig 41). In due time the heads were replaced by the LNER standard rectangular lamp case having a danger aspect of an enamelled white disc with a horizontal red stripe (figs 4 & 42). Subsequently the LNER added a second striped disc for clear, this latter stripe for clear being tilted at 45 degrees. Here memory deserts me, for I cannot recall one of these at Firsby, though I saw them elsewhere. Eventually all the discs at Firsby were changed to the final LNER version, in which a single enamelled white disc with a red stripe tilted through 45 degrees like a banner signal, and these appear in many of the pictures, for example figs 18, 32, and 33.

43 Disc No. 41 in 1947, still the same format as seen in fig 42, but with the mechanism mounted the other way, so that the operating wire pulls on the balance weight crank and not on the base plate. The head of course has been turned through 180 degrees on the spindle so that it faces the correct direction!

Before closing this section the level crossing deserves a mention. I know of no similar one [but having said that reports to the contrary will pour in!]. It is believed to have replaced the former pair of hand operated gates when the road was widened. Its double set of gates were operated by a handwheel in the signalbox, interlocked with the lever frame; a necessary refinement not found in most of the East Lincolnshire line signalboxes, but imagine the performance if the signalman had had to descend the box steps to open and close half a dozen gates! The main line gates overlapped in the closed position, because of the angle of the crossing (fig 45). The two half gates of No. 1 set, hung at the obtuse angle, had only just enough clearance as they swung across the short diagonal, whereas the full gates of No. 2 set, on the long diagonal, had plenty of clearance (figs 44 & 46). Because of their large angular swing the half gates were operated by rack and pinion, the remaining four by the usual half cranks. To open or close the gates two 'winds' of the wheel were required, which earned the signalman double marks. The first wind was anticlockwise. I found this a little awkward but with practice the knack was acquired of winding anticlockwise with the left hand. No. 1 set - the two half gates and the inner Skegness line gate - required a long wind the full length of the lead screw of the winding mechanism. The three heavy full gates of No. 2 set were quite difficult to get on the move, but only needed a comparatively short wind. This feature was used as part of the interlocking. Only when the gates were fully closed was the operating linkage, and the tappet bar attached to it, at the forward end of the lead screw with the notch of the tappet in line with the dog of the miniature lever on the winding frame, allowing that lever to be reversed to lock the wheel and release appropriate signals.

44 The gates closing seen from the footbridge. No 2 set is half closed and the signalman can be seen in the Box winding away with his left hand; as the first wind is always anticlockwise it is often easier to use the left hand. It will be seen that the iron suspension rods for the Skegness line gates remain the older type anchored to the top rail of the gate, whereas the newer gates by the main line have a two-bar suspension anchored to the lower rail of the gate; moreover the outer gate at the right of the picture has no extension bar - see fig 45. Note, too, the Signal Box access gate, similar in construction to the pedestrian crossing handgates, a replacement for the all-wooden one seen in fig 15 chapter 2.

45 A 1936 shot of the down side gates which shows the way they overlap when closed, and in particular the iron extension bar bolted to the end of the large gate. When the gates were open this bar overlapped the end of the middle half gate of No. 1 set. No extension bar was fitted to the corresponding gate by the up line, nor to the replacement gate, see fig 44.

46 The second wind in the sequence of closing the gates: No. 1 set is being closed. Less awkward as the second wind is clockwise. With No. 2 set closed the linkage seen on the outer gates has swivelled the red warning lamps so that they correctly point along the road.

47 A view of the level crossing from the Irby road side, that is with the Skegness line nearest the camera, No. 2 set of gates is closing. What a pity the motorist must needs choose that instant to get out of the car and obscure the *Beware of the Trains* notice. Near the far end of the houses along the left of the road is the house occupied by Mr. Cash, coal merchant (chapter 7). It is the one whose roof is at right angles to the road. Just beyond it on the same side of the road is the cottage in which I lived for 17 years.

48 From the down side looking towards Irby, again with No. 2 set closing, this view shows the gate stops raised in the road and the two-bar suspension of the large gate. Almost in the centre of the picture in the middle distance is a long black wooden building, officially entitled 'Firsby Parish Hall', but known universally as 'Firsby Hut'. I well remember the children's Christmas parties held in the Hut, when Father Christmas would arrive - not on a reindeer-hauled sleigh, but on a 4-wheeler LNER luggage barrow from the station hauled by stalwart station staff.

49 The signalman opening the gates. The wheel release lever has been pushed back, No. 54 pulled to reverse the stops to No. 1 set which is being wound, wheel anticlockwise, the die block moving to the left of the picture. When fully wound, the gate changeover lever No. 56 will be pulled and the stops to No. 2 set (No. 55) pulled; then No. 2 set can be opened, short wind clockwise.

To end this chapter it may be of interest to describe the sequence of operation of the gates. In the closed position (for trains to pass) the miniature lever is reversed, and levers 54, 55, & 56 normal.

The opening sequence is:-

No. 54 reversed to operate the gate stops of No. 1 set.
The miniature lever returned normal to unlock the wheel.
No. 1 set (two half gates and Skegness line inner gate) is wound: wheel anticlockwise, long wind the full length of the lead screw. (fig 49).
No. 56 reversed to change the mechanism to No. 2 set.
No. 55 reversed to operate the gate stops of No. 2 set.
No. 2 set (three full gates, - two main line and Skegness line outer gate) is wound: wheel clockwise, short wind a little over half the length of the lead screw.

50 Closing the gates. No. 2 set has been closed - the die block is at the extreme left of the lead screw and No. 55 (stops to No. 2 set) normal. The gate changeover lever, No. 56, is being pushed normal, then No. 54 (stops to No. 1 set) will be restored normal and No. 1 set closed, long wind clockwise, the die block moving to the right the full length of the lead screw, and finally the miniature lever on the winding frame, hidden in the photograph by the movement of lever No. 56, can be pulled to lock the wheel and release appropriate signals.

The closing sequence is almost, but not quite, the reverse of the foregoing:-

No. 55, stops of No. 2 set, restored to normal.
No. 2 set closed, short wind, wheel anticlockwise.
No. 56 restored to normal to change the mechanism to No. 1 set. (fig 50).
No. 54, stops of No. 1 set, restored to normal.
No. 1 set closed, long wind, wheel clockwise.
The miniature lever on the winding frame reversed to lock the wheel.

CHAPTER 4

BOSTON, SPALDING, PETERBOROUGH, & LONDON

How well I remember hearing that cry at Firsby around about 10 in the morning and 2 in the afternoon, and what an aura of importance it conjured up in the youthful mind! A train (or part of it anyway) going through to the Capital, with roofboards proclaimimg *Kings Cross Grimsby and Cleethorpes.* And to crown it all, hauled by none other than one of the famous Ivatt large Atlantics, whose exploits were so well known. These fine engines, resplendant in lined LNER green, were always firm favourites of mine, and it is no coincidence that one is the subject of my first railway photograph (fig 1). This was 4409 on the '2 express' at New Year 1936. The 4-cylinder rebuild, 3279, was transferred to New England in 1935 and was a regular on this train, and returned to it after it was rebuilt a second time to a 2-cylinder engine (fig 55). I also have a note of 4429 on the morning '10 express', 4418 on the 9 pm up mail, and 4408, 3282, & 3285 on the 4 pm down local: they would return on the mail.

The Atlantics we saw on the expresses were based at New England, and there were three out and home turns through Firsby in the thirties. The first came down on the mail and newspaper express leaving Peterborough about three in the morning and calling at Firsby at about 4-30; this engine returned with the express from Cleethorpes which called at Firsby at about 10 am. The second turn was the 8-30 am (at Firsby) down stopping train, returning in the afternoon with the '2 express'. The third Atlantic turn also came down with a stopping train calling at Firsby at about 4 pm, and came up with the night mail which called at Firsby at 9 pm. This mail was a regular weekday train for over a century, and in the late 1860s it was the fastest run on the East Lincolnshire Railway, taking a little over 2 and a quarter hours for the journey from Grimsby to Peterborough, a schedule little changed a century later!

In the nineteenth century, except for the mail, most trains in Lincolnshire were slow, and in the late 1880s there were complaints about the poor service to Grimsby. At that time through coaches between Grimsby and London were exchanged between the GNR and M S & L at Retford. By the early part of the twentieth century, though, the fast, limited stop trains had appeared on the East Lincolnshire between Grimsby and Peterborough, and these trains called at Firsby at more or less the same times each day from then on. Up to the 1930s they were through carriages rather than through London trains, the London portion being attached at Peterborough to a main line train from the north or to a train from Cromer to London via the M & GN. The afternoon train was often ten coaches or more over the East Lincolnshire section, of which about half went to London, giving rise at Firsby to the call *Boston, Spalding, & Peterborough, London only in the rear!* It was economies after 1939 affecting the main line connection which gave us our own complete train to London, the morning 10 express, which from then on remained an independent through train from Cleethorpes to London. But the same war-time economies resulted in the discontinuance of the through London coaches on the 2 express, never to be restored except on selected occasions, and finally the Grimsby-Peterborough train degenerated into a two car diesel unit.

In the down direction there was but one through portion from London; this was detached from the 4 pm (approx) main line express from Kings Cross, and worked forward from Peterborough calling at Firsby at about 7 pm. This was the first to become an independent train during the 1930s, and so it continued thenceforward to the end. It was worked over the East Lincolnshire line from Boston by an Immingham engine and men, usually an ex-GCR 4-4-0 of class D9. The engine worked up to Boston on the stopping train which called at Firsby at 4-15 pm or thereabouts (fig 123). These engines put up some good performances on this turn, for the express was no lightweight. I remember a day in April 1937 on which the fifteen and a quarter miles from Boston to Firsby were run in 18 minutes start to stop. This was a good effort for a modest 4-4-0, bearing in mind the speed restriction for the first three quarters of a mile out of Boston which would occupy about two of those 18 minutes.

With traffic increasing an additional express was introduced in the 1930s to and from Grimsby to connect at Peterborough with London expresses and which gave a fast overall journey time. In the up direction it called at Firsby at around 8 am, and at 9-45 pm on the return run in the evening. It began as

TABLE 1

FIRSBY - BOSTON

Date	11-6-62 (Whit Mon)	18-6-62
Train	6-9 pm	9-42 am express
Engine No.	61364	70040
Engine Name	-	Clive of India
Load	11	11 inc buffet
Tare (est tons)	370	375
	m.p.h.	*m.p.h.*
Firsby dep	*2 late*	*RT*
R Steeping	10 (slack)	20 (slack)
Bellwater Jct	50	50
East Ville		53
MP 116	53	
MP 115	58	
Old Leake	61½	60
	then 62½	
Sibsey	61½	58½
High Ferry	62½	
Boston arr *(min)*	22	*21*
Sched min	22	*21*

a featherweight train of two coaches only, hauled by a big ex-GCR 4-6-0 of Immingham shed! Immingham's allocation of 4-6-0 classes was noted for its variety, and so we saw an interesting selection of engines on this train. The tiny express with a big engine soon earned itself the nickname *Flying Flea,* after a small private aeroplane put on the market at about that time. So popular did the *Flea* become that it had grown into a substantial buffet car train by 1939, and after war-time absence it returned as a full length buffet car express right through to Kings Cross. And so the *Flying Flea* continued to the end, far outliving the long forgotten aeroplane that gave it its nickname. It is of interest that for over 20 years following the demise of the East Lincolnshire line what may be regarded as the 'ghost' of the *Flying Flea* still ran between Grimsby and Kings Cross, but via Newark, using a specially-built loop between the former LNER and Midland lines.

The end of the war saw the beginning of the Thompson B1 inundation of the LNER, and of course these new engines appeared on both the *Flea* and the expresses (and nearly everything else in Lincolnshire too). Gradually Immingham B1s took over the expresses, working through to Kings Cross, changing crews at Boston, and although a B1 in good form was not to be looked down upon, they found the going rather hard over the main line south of Peterborough, especially in summer. I have no log of a B1 on the expresses, but to give an idea of what a B1 in good form could do, on Whit Monday 11 June 1962 the 6-9 pm up train was extended to Kings Cross, and 61374 took the packed 11-coach train from Firsby to Boston in the booked time of 22 minutes, attaining 62 m.p.h. between Old Leake and High Ferry (col 1 of Table 1).

Then in early 1961 Britannias, displaced from the Great Eastern lines by diesels, arrived at Immingham for use on the London trains (figs 52 & 57). They represented a significant increase in power. Table 1 column 2 shows an up run with the morning express, while Table 2 shows some down runs on the 7 pm arrival at Firsby. The best was Thursday 2 August 1962 when 70038 took only eighteen and a half minutes to bring 11 coaches from Boston to Firsby with a steady 69-70 m.p.h. from East Ville until checked at Bellwater. The train was well patronised, denying me a suitable vantage point from which to observe, hence the lack of detail in the log. The other two runs, earlier in the season with lighter loads, were nontheless good, for the bridge repair slack at the River Steeping would cost some running time.

But the reign of the Britannias was all too brief, for with the start of the summer timetable in May of 1963 Kings Cross closed to steam, and the inevitable diesels took over. At first it was the smaller Brush type 2 (now class 31), which, like the B1s before them, found the going a bit hard. And so the larger Brush type 4 (now class 47) were put on to perform the last act of the show.

TABLE 2

EVENING DOWN EXPRESS (arr FIRSBY 7 pm)

Date	5-6-62	14-6-62	2-8-62
Engine No.	700041	70039	70038
Engine Name	Sir John Moore	Sir Christopher Wren	Robin Hood
Load	8 inc buffet	8 inc buffet	11 inc buffet
Tare (est tons)	285	285	375
Boston dep	*RT*	*RT*	*RT*
	m.p.h	*m.p.h.*	*m.p.h.*
MP 111	60½	62½	
High Ferry	61½	62½	
Sibsey	63½	64½	
Old Leake	65½	69	66
MP 115	67-70		
MP 116	69		
East Ville	70	64	69
			69-70 until
Bellwater Jct	70	60 (sigs?)	50 (sigs?)
R Steeping	10*	20*	
Firsby arr (min)	*19*	*20m 30 s*	*18m 30s*
Sched min	*21*	*21*	*21*

* bridge repair slack

51 The morning London express from Cleethorpes at the beginning of BR in early 1948. A B1 engine resplendent in LNER green, but with BR lettering and number. Really an LNER train, made up of Gresley coaches. This picture is also of interest for its rear view of the three-arm signal, No. 34, 37, 23. This was a running signal controlling passenger traffic and not a shunt signal: in fact in former times it was a tall bracket signal with full size arms and located at the foot of the down platform ramp by the crossing.

52 The morning London express in 1962, during the brief reign of the Britannias. Here we have 70038 *Robin Hood* on August Bank Holiday drawn forward to bring the rear half of the train to the platform. The Spilsby line can be seen curving away to the right, although by this time it was reduced to a refuge siding extending only as far as Barton's crossing about half a mile away.

53 The afternoon express with through coaches for Kings Cross at New Year 1936 - the second of my railway photographs, taken immediately after fig 1. Great Northern Atlantic No. 4409 is setting off for Boston. Of particular interest are the leading coaches, the then nearly new steel-panelled (but still teak framed) coaches introduced in 1935 for the East Lincolnshire sevices. They were in sets of five, all side corridors. The middle vehicle was a first/third composite, flanked either end by an articulated twin comprising a third class and a brake/third.

54 In the last year of the LNER, 1947, clean green Immingham engine 1142 at the platform with the afternoon express from Grimsby to Peterborough calling at Firsby at 1-47 pm, though now without the through London coaches. Suspended as a wartime economy measure, the through coaches were never restored.

55 Not an express, but the 8-30 am down stopping train in the late summer of 1938; Atlantic 3279 back in service from New England on its regular duty: down with this train and returning with the 1-47 pm express conveying through coaches for London. I well remember this engine on this duty regularly as both a 4-cylinder and a 2-cylinder engine from the time it was sent to New England in 1935.

56 Immingham B1 No. 1082 on the down 7 pm express in the late summer of 1947. Having drawn forward to bring the rear part of the train to the platform it awaits the right away. This was a daily practice in the summer, when the expresses regularly loaded to a dozen coaches, often more in LNER days.

57 The down 7 pm express with Britannia Pacific 70038 *Robin Hood* of Immingham arriving at Firsby on Saturday 4 August 1962. This train also appears in fig 25.

CHAPTER 5

FISH FOR LONDON

Grimsby and its docks being the territory of the Manchester, Sheffield & Lincolnshire Railway, that company quickly became a leading fish carrier, with daily trains to many main cities. There was one notable exception, London, for the nineteenth century M S & L had no line to the capital city. Moreover by the time the M S & L line to Grimsby and its docks was open for traffic, the East Lincolnshire Railway to Boston and the GNR line thence to London were open, and in 1851 the GNR obtained an Act of Parliament giving it access to Grimsby docks and sidings for fish and goods traffic. So from the beginning Firsby saw its daily London-bound fish trains, and the returning empties, a traffic which continued almost without a break until the East Lincolnshire line was marked for closure by BR. Even when in the twentieth century the newly styled Great Central Railway opened its line to Marylebone the East Lincolnshire and GNR route from Grimsby to London was more direct. The GCR did in fact try to divert the London fish trains to their new route, but the Great Northern obtained an injunction to retain their traditional traffic, and so the London-bound fish trains continued to come through Firsby, though the GCR did operate their own Grimsby-Marylebone fish train service until the 1923 grouping when the new LNER promptly routed all the Grimsby fish for London via East Lincolnshire and the GNR route. Two trains ran daily, passing through Firsby in the evening at about 7 pm and 8 pm. The 4-wheel vans were kept for this traffic, and returned empty to Grimsby each day; one empty train I remember running through in mid afternoon. By the 1930s a few bogie vans began to appear in the trains' formation By the 1960s the increase in popularity of frozen food caused the pattern to change. The two ordinary fish trains (and returning empties) still ran but they became shorter, and were supplemented by trains of refrigerated containers on charter to the frozen food firms. And in addition to the dedicated fish trains, it was a long standing practice to attach individual vans of fish to passenger trains for relatively local destinations, such as Skegness or Boston, though by the 1960s this local traffic was being lost to road competition.

The fast transit necessary for fish would be no problem to the Great Northern, for that company had always appreciated the importance of an express goods service. It is likely, then, that a variety of the GNR mixed traffic locomotive classes would have been seen charging through Firsby with the fish trains, among them almost certainly members of Mr. Stirling's 0-4-2 class built during the latter half of the nineteenth century. A notable development occurred in 1920 with the appearance of No. 1000, the first of Mr. Gresley's 3-cylinder 2-6-0 fast goods engines of class K3. This engine was sent new to New England, and was immediately put to work on the main fish train, coming north with the empties which passed through Firsby in mid afternoon, and returning through Firsby at 7 pm with the main fish train for London, which it took all the way. Within a few months No. 1000 was joined at New England by other members of the class, and from then on for almost 40 years the Grimsby-London fish workings were virtually monopolised by the K3s until their mass withdrawal in 1960-62. A rare instance of a brand new locomotive class taking charge of trains through Firsby, something which may well not have happened since the opening of the line in 1848. These trains, their vans swaying as they sped through with scant regard for the nominal 60 m.p.h. speed limit for 4-wheelers, remain an unforgettable sight and sound of early childhood, and the K3s have been firm favourites ever since. They frequently hauled substantial loads, often 80 or so vans; 100 and over were occasionally noted on the '7 fish' which was usually the heavier of the two trains. The later '8 fish' generally loaded to about 20 fewer vans. Occasionally, at busy holiday times, the procession of return trips from Skegness would cause the fish to be held in Firsby station, and it was on one such occasion that the driver, seeing the writer (and his younger brother) watching from the opposite platform, climbed down to the track and treated us to a clear and concise explanation of the working of the engine, pointing out the function of each part of the valve gear. Of course the fish trains were too fast for the box Brownie though the enthusiastic youthful photographer had to make just one attempt and learn the hard way! Fortunately the better camera obtained later secured a few shots before the K3s disappeared for ever (figs 58 & 59).

As with the express trains after the war, so also the working of the fish trains was transferred from New England to Immingham, where a number of K3s were already based, and these engines carried on the good work through the 1950s, running through to London, now with a change of crew at Boston. A few withdrawals took place during 1959, thereafter more rapidly until the last K3s went in December 1962. Immingham still had a couple in November of that year, but by 1959 BR standard 2-10-0s were based there, and these engines began to be used on the fish trains. For a short while one of the inevitable B1s was rostered, though the B1 was not as strong as the K3. Indeed, a brand new New England B1 was noted as early as 1947-8 on the down fish empties: perhaps there was no K3 available on that occasion and New England decided (or were told) to try the new engine. And in 1963 Immingham Britannias had a fish turn. But the BR 2-10-0s were the real successors to the K3s, and they represented a significant increase in tractive power over the K3, and also, like the K3, could run fast. So it was these hefty engines that saw out steam working on the fish trains, and proved worthy successors to the long and distinguished reign of the K3s. But it did not last long, for after 1964 when the East Lincolnshire line was scheduled for closure the fish trains were re-routed, and doubtless diesels took over until the traffic was lost to the railway altogether.

58 The fish train as I remember it: the 7 pm up in the summer of 1947 with one of the faithful K3s in charge passing the North Box. The engine, left hand drive and having a stepped out tender, is probably one of the ten built in 1925 by Darlington, or one of their 1924 batch that were later converted to left hand drive. Note the painting style used for the name board before nationalization compared with that depicted in fig 27 (see also caption to fig 22).

59 Still active in BR days, 61956 approaching the station about 6-30 pm on 13 June 1957. Of interest is the shunt signal, No. 4 of the North Box, perched on a post so as to be visible from the Skegness line round the grassy bank. The original disc, rotating on a vertical spindle, had a normal mechanism on the ground as usual with a tall spindle to carry the head, not easy with a tilting banner.

60 It is the last day of July 1963, all the K3s have gone, and 70039 *Sir Christopher Wren* finds a job hauling the 7 pm up fish train, having himself been displaced from the expresses by diesels. Note the handwheel operated control valve for the water crane, - and the chalked instructions on the column! The handwheel replaced the original lifting handle control which appears in fig 127 taken in 1948.

61 A B1 being tried out on the down fish empties in 1948. An early intrusion into the traditional domain of the K3s. The signalman, Mr. Musgrove, (in shirt sleeves) watches from the box doorway; the man with him is probably Mr. Cargill, the relief signalman at the South.

62 Steam's last word on the fish trains. A BR standard 2-10-0 goods engine, 92202 of Immingham, passing the South Box at about 6-30 pm on Bank Holiday 3 August 1964.

CHAPTER 6

IRONSTONE FOR FRODINGHAM

Firsby might not be thought of as a likely place to see trains of iron ore passing through, and it certainly was not in the mind of the line's promoters in 1848. However, it eventually came to pass, albeit not until the latter days of the LNER. The origins of this traffic go back to before the grouping, so perhaps a few words will be of interest.

The ironstone came from mines around Colsterworth, six miles south of Grantham on the Great North Road, where in 1916 the Frodingham Iron and Steel Company commenced mining. The GNR served these workings by means of a branch from High Dyke near the north portal of Stoke tunnel. Initially the ore trains and the returning empties used the main line to Doncaster, and thence the GCR line to Frodingham. In the 1930s they were re-routed, leaving the main line at Barkston, and travelling via Honington, Lincoln, and Barnetby, reversing at both Lincoln and Barnetby. At Lincoln these heavy trains had to make their way over three busy level crossings to reverse, and then return over the same three crossings to gain the former GCR line to Barnetby. The whole performance was repeated, of course, by the returning empties. As road traffic increased the congestion caused became serious, and again the route was changed. Still leaving the main line at Barkston, the trains now ran via Boston and the East Lincolnshire line to Grimsby and thence via Barnetby to Frodingham, and so for the first time they could travel from High Dyke to Frodingham without reversal - or even without a stop! One cannot help wondering why, when the whole operation came under one control after grouping, this East Lincolnshire route was not used much earlier.

Initially one train per day sufficed, with reliefs run as required, but by the time the trains were running via Lincoln there were two regular daily trains. Demand increased steadily until by 1939 there were three or sometimes four trains daily, each conveying up to 700 tons of ore. But after the war-time boom two trains sufficed once more. In LNER days specially built hopper wagons were used, and kept for this traffic only, returning as empty trains to High Dyke. Later on the hoppers were replaced by flat-sided all-steel tippler wagons, doubtless in response to revised ore handling plant at Frodingham, and it is the tipplers which appear in our pictures.

Between the wars the service was in the hands of the Robinson 2-8-0s of class O4, which had been a familiar sight at Firsby on other types of goods trains during that period. But by the time the ironstone trains came to use the East Lincolnshire line the Gresley 3-cylinder class O2 had taken over, and these fine engines put in some sterling work until their demise at the end of 1963. So as steam had its final fling on the ironstone trains Firsby resounded to the stirring sight and sound of the Gresley beat of these engines working hard to the end of their days, and some pictures of them just had to be included in this book.

But of course it couldn't last. By 1964, because they wanted to close the East Lincolnshire line, BR were reverting to a Lincoln route for the ironstone. In anticipation of authority for the closure a new curve had been built at some expense to link the East Coast Main Line at Newark with the former Midland line to Lincoln, and by using it reversal at Lincoln was now avoided. And by this time the worst of the level crossings at Lincoln, Pelham Street, had been replaced by a bridge. Reversal at Barnetby was again required as in former years, but in the anxiety to close the East Lincolnshire line it appears that this was overlooked. However, not many years had passed before the Colsterworth mines became worked out, and so an interesting part of Lincolnshire railway operation came to an end.

Figs 63-66. *The Gresley beat on the High Dyke & Frodingham Ironstone trains on Friday 30 August 1963 as the Class O2 engines work hard to the end of their days.*

63 Passing the North Box about 4 pm with a return train of empty wagons for High Dyke is 63981. A mere 20 years old, this engine lasted until November.

64 Another 20 year old with 3 months to go, 63984 makes a fine sight from the bank beside the Skegness line as it storms past the Station Box at 2 pm with its train of well loaded ore wagons.

65 A month from withdrawal the 30 year old 63960 hauls its load of ore towards Firsby at 9 o'clock in the morning.

66 Returning with empty wagons later that morning is 40 year old 63942 pulling away from the station towards the South. This engine, too, had only a month to go.

67 An unusual engine on an ironstone train on 18 August 1960. Boston class K2 engine No. 61742 is seen passing the Station Box. Perhaps there was some trouble with the booked engine and the driver asked for a substitute when he reached Boston. As I remember the engine was pulling along at quite a good pace making a lovely sound.

68 Foreshadowing the departure of the Gresley class O2s, Austerity 90602 is in charge of an ore train south of the station in mid-morning 30 August 1963.

CHAPTER 7

GOODS TRAINS

It has been said that the fast expresses attracted the glamour and attention, but the goods train - and the almost universal 0-6-0 workhorse - earned the profits. Two types of goods traffic through Firsby - fish and ironstone - are mentioned in their own chapters: here we recall some other goods trains.

There were a number of through workings. I recall an early down goods going through about 6 am; there was also one each way during the morning and afternoon, and to end the day the last train of all was the up "midnight goods" which ran through about 10-45 or so, and which I occasionally observed illicitly from our bedroom window! This last was, I believe, usually hauled by an ex-GNR engine, probably a J6 or J1, or a D2 4-4-0. Of course at that time of night it was but a silhouette, and it is the remembrance of its sound that is my guide. Of the day-time runs, one up and one down were regularly hauled by those tough and reliable 2-8-0 engines, the ex-GCR "Tinies", which could be found all over the LNER. The ones through Firsby were probably from Immingham or (after 1932) Frodingham on through workings to and from Whitemoor. I have notes of engines 5393 and 6362 on these turns: the latter was one of the engines built for the War Department during 1914-1918 and bought later by the LNER. The Tinies were still active through Firsby in the 1950s (fig 70). Occasionally seen on these workings were the ex-GCR 0-8-0 type, which looked like a Tiny with a pair of wheels missing! I have a note of 5151 going through on the down. These 0-8-0 turns were probably Frodingham workings, for until the new shed was built there in 1932 Frodingham was dependent on Keadby, and the 0-8-0 was the longest engine that Keadby could cope with. Other engines on through goods were the excellent J39 class of 0-6-0 (2783, 2966, & 2967 were noted); there were also Gresley K2s (fig 78), and I have one note of a B5, No. 5181. After 1943 a new generation of War Department engines began to appear in the shape of "austerity" 2-8-0s, and, echoing the 1920s, the LNER purchased a number of these engines when hostilities ceased. Many more were acquired by BR, and they turned up quite often on through workings (fig 69).

69 A down part fitted goods running through the station in the morning of Wednesday 29 July 1964, with Austerity 2-8-0 No. 90133. Like the LNER in the 1920s, BR purchased a number of war surplus engines from the Ministry of Supply. Formerly this one - then WD 7037 - had been on loan to the LNER for 21 months during 1943-4 before being sent overseas.

For general goods the maid-of-all-work was the 0-6-0, and one result of grouping was the appearance of ex-GCR "pom-poms" (class J11) on goods trains through Firsby: engines of this class I noted were 5210, 5214, 5243, 5997, 6116. Naturally various ex-GNR classes were used, mostly the popular J6: I have a record of 3532, 3579, 3591, 3598 of that class. The J6s, and their J1 and J2 companions often turned up on passenger trains, especially excursions. In complete contrast, Ivatt high-wheeled passenger 4-4-0s of classes D2 and D3 took turns on goods, including quite often pick-up goods (fig 73). All these classes were still active after the war and into BR days (figs 71, 72, 74, 77). In 1947 ex-GCR Atlantics came to Lincolnshire and these appeared too (fig 12). Then in BR days ex-LMS 2-6-0s were sent to Boston, and of course there were the inevitable B1s (figs 75, 80). Finally BR standard 2-10-0s put in appearances on fitted goods (fig 81).

It was during the afternoon that the various pick up goods trains called at Firsby, with one exception. This odd man out was the Skegness goods. It arrived from Boston around 6 am, and shunted in Firsby yard before setting off for Skegness. Its return trip was in the afternoon. In the 1930s the return run at about 3-30 pm was sent round the curve to the South. This meant that after his mid-day shift in the Station Box Mr. Roberts had a daily walk to open the South for the Skegness goods, and this arrangement continued thenceforward to the end. Around the middle of the day the New Line Lincoln goods would arrive (fig 12); after sorting its wagons it would leave again in the early afternoon on the return run to Lincoln. Along the East Lincolnshire "main line" a pick up goods in each direction called at Firsby in the afternoon, and there was also the Spilsby line goods. This last was a Spilsby-Firsby-Spilsby round trip fitted in between the passenger run to Spilsby after

70 A down goods passing the Station Box in the morning sunshine of 1 August 1963, in fact it looks like two engineering trains put together! The engine is 2-8-0 No. 63913 of Staveley Central shed, originally class O5, re-boilered in 1936 to become class O4.

71 In 1947 D2 engines were still in use on goods. Here No. 2154 (old 4324) is taking a part fitted through goods past the up platform late on a sunny afternoon. This picture makes an interesting comparison with fig 3.

72 No. 64191, one of the popular GNR general purpose goods engines, LNER class J6, here seen on an up part fitted goods on 17 June 1954. These engines were equally at home on passenger as on goods trains, and were often seen on excursions going round the curve to Skegness (fig 85).

meeting the up Cleethorpes express at 2 pm and the 3-30 pm departure from Spilsby to meet the 4 pm trains at Firsby. The Spilsby engine would quite often carry out shunting while at Firsby. I seem to recall this happening early in the morning for the 8-45 to Spilsby which took us to school was often a mixed train, - and made us late because of shunting at Halton.

Almost all types of goods traffic was handled at Firsby - from coal to cattle; fertilisers to furniture vans; minerals to machinery; in fact anything that could be conveyed in a goods train. On the up side by the loop which ran from the bay platform behind the North Box to the up sidings (and known as the crow from its whistle code) was the livestock pen, (fig 18), where a fair amount of livestock was dealt with in the old days when the railway was the accepted form of transport, but by the 1930s more and more people were investing in road vans and the livestock business began to fall. But on the other side of the line the goods shed was busy with general merchandise, larger items being dealt with in the open where there was a hand operated crane capable of lifting surprisingly heavy loads when wound by four strong men and true.

At Firsby there were two coal merchants. Mr. Marriott's house and yard backed on to the railway on the up side, where there was a private coal siding the buffer stops of which were right by his boundary fence. Handy one might think, but to take his lorry from his yard to the coal siding required a drive of a quarter of a mile or more, along his own drive to the road, along the road to the station, and then along the up yard approach drive behind the pump house and

73 A down pick up goods at about 3-30 pm in 1936, with a GNR 4-4-0, No. 4397 of class D2. The tail of this train can be seen in the distance in fig 15, and one of its wagons fortuitously appears in fig 45. With enough imagination it is just possible to discern the shadowy figure of Mr. Easter, the signalman, in the Box. This is also a useful view of the three arm-signal; beside it on the short post is the wooden case in which was installed the electric lock operated by the Spilsby line train staff to release the lowest arm (No. 23) for the Spilsby train to depart. This view from the footbridge makes an interesting comparison with that of fig 16, taken a quarter of a century later.

cattle pen! As a child I often wondered why he did not have a gap and gate set in the fence for direct access! In fact I believe that at one time the coal siding did extend into Mr. Marriott's yard, but from the appearance of the ground and the fence as I remember it between the wars that must have been a very long time ago.

The other coal merchant, Mr. G. Cash, had his house and yard next door but one to the cottage where my family lived (fig 47). Less up-to-date than Mr. Marriott, Mr. Cash had a four-wheel low-sided dray which was hauled by his white horse, called Sunny, who spent its off-duty hours grazing in the field between Mr. Cash's house and the railway. Wagons of coal for Mr. Cash were delivered to the down siding, from whence he had to cart it up to his yard, but quite often he would weigh and bag up direct fron the wagons to go out on his round. Mr. Cash was quite a character, he lived alone, and he is the only person I've seen use a hammer and cold chisel to open a tin of bully beef, the tin held in a large engineer's vice! Along the top of the sides of his dray were narrow horizontal ledges, and upon these Mr. Cash would perform a quite involved little dance for the entertainment of any children he might encounter on his round. Sunny, of course, knew the round as well as did Mr. Cash, and ambled on regardless of the lack of guiding hand on the reins or of Mr. Cash's antics on the ledges of the dray.

Firsby certainly was busy in those days. Goods, parcels, etc. were delivered and collected over a wide area by road from Firsby station and yard. I can remember the blue LNER motor vehicles; also the articulated units known appropriately as "mechanical horses" which operated from Firsby in the 1930s. With their detachable trailer section the "horse" would be out on one collection/delivery round while a second trailer was loaded in the yard. The tractor unit was a quite compact three-wheel chassis, and being jointed in the middle the complete unit was very flexible and could turn in a small space.

During 1939-45 Firsby goods yard made its own contribution to the war effort, for large quantities of building materials were brought in for the construction of the military airfields at Great Steeping and East Kirkby. And when the construction work was complete, there were regular arrivals of wagon loads of bombs to be dealt with, - another traffic never dreamed of by the railway's promoters.

74 A "pom-pom", No. 64284, passing the Station Box on a down through goods on 18 August 1960, the signalman, my good friend Mr. Easter, leaning over the signalbox rail exchanging messages with the enginemen.

By 1946 both coal merchants' businesses had gone, the goodwill acquired by merchants at Wainfleet and Skegness, and soon the new owners ceased to use Firsby yard. The coal siding was taken up, and Firsby had lost a colourful character. However, Firsby was still listed as a coal station. The Railway Clearing House handbook of stations for 1956 (a foolscap volume about an inch and a quarter thick) quotes Firsby as offering a full range of services, viz:- parcels and miscellaneous items by passenger train; general goods, coal, minerals, and wagonload traffic; furniture vans, carriages, cars, portable engines and machines on wheels(!); livestock; horse boxes and prize cattle vans. The handbook also gave the capacity of Firsby's crane as 30 cwt. but I feel sure the crane must have lifted more than that on occasions, for example an agricultural implement, or a door-to-door container. Oh yes, there were containers all that long ago!

And so the pattern of goods services continued in BR days, except for the Spilsby line of course. For when the passenger service was suspended in September 1939 the engine and men were transferred to Boston, and so the Spilsby goods service operated in reverse as it were from the Firsby end, which continued until final closure of the Spilsby line in 1958. But with no coal traffic, and with road competition, which had already taken the livestock business, becoming more and more serious after the ending of fuel rationing, Firsby yard was never as busy as in pre-war days. Then came the Beeching plan, and by the summer of 1963 the down sidings had been cut short and Nos, 10 and 12 points at the North removed. And during that summer, too, the chair-borne railwaymen at the London head office were collecting statistics and hatching their plots for the East Lincolnshire closure, which they issued in May of 1964, and strengthened their case by withdrawing goods services at the end of that year.

75 An example of the universal use of the B1 class: 61365 on a through goods on the up line between the station and the South mid-morning Friday 30 August 1963.

76 A down empty wagon train in 1947 at No. 57 crossing near the South junction in charge of No. 3911, one of the excellent 2-8-0 of class O4.

77 The afternoon up pick up goods at the South in 1947, in charge of 5017 (old 3073), one of ten express goods engines turned out by Ivatt in 1912. They became LNER class J2.

78 (left upper) Taken about 5 pm on the same day in 1936 as figs 15, 73, & 123, the pioneer Gresley 2-6-0 takes an up part fitted goods through the station. Originally numbered 1630, it was the first of the ten engines of class K1, which were superseded by the larger-boilered K2. By the time this picture was taken the K1s had all been equipped with the larger boiler making them class K2, and 1630 had become 4630.

79 (left lower) The Skegness goods. Displaying pickup goods headlamps Immingham B1 No. 61003 *Gazelle* comes round past No. 13 signal on the single line from the station to the East on its way calling at all stations to Skegness at about 9 o'clock on Saturday morning 1 August 1964. On the return run from Skegness to Boston no calls are paid so the train runs as unfitted through goods (figs 28 & 120). It was here, about where the photographer was standing, that the original route of the village road crossed the Skegness branch; the gatehouse was to the left off the picture, and for many years was the home of my signalman friend Mr. Easter. (See also fig 99.) The opening of the south curve introduced another level crossing close by, see caption to fig 91.

80 (opposite upper) An Ivatt 2-6-0, No. 43044, in charge of an up fitted goods passing through the station at about 5-15 pm on Thursday 29 August 1963. Of interest is the view of the stump of the pump house chimney - with weeds growing out of it! I noticed its absence on returning after the war; presumably it was taken down for fear that it might be a danger to aircraft. The steam engines had already been superseded by electric power, mains electricity having arrived at that end of Firsby in 1938.

81 (opposite lower) BR 2-10-0 No. 92196 in August 1964 on the up working shown in fig 80 in the hands of the Ivatt 2-6-0 a year earlier. Another goods is going through on the down, and, crouching on the platform, the writer's late brother-in-law is filming the cushioning of the wagon buffers as the train slows down. On the up platform to the right of the engine can be seen the cast iron lamp standard. Though supporting a 1938 electric fitting in place of the original gas lantern the standard itself may well be that provided by the East Lincolnshire company for the opening in 1848. A similar standard was located by the fence on the down platform opposite, and - prior to the provision of electric light in 1938 - there was a third one by the handgate at the Skegness line side.

82 At the north entrance to the goods shed the engine of the afternoon pick up goods - having set its train back into one of the up sidings - is collecting wagons to add to the train. The driver watches from the cab lookout as the shunter engages the hook of his shunting pole with the hanging link to couple the wagons to the engine.

83 The engine has drawn the wagons out from the goods shed siding and propelled them over the top crossover to the up line. He now comes forward on the down line to cross to the up line by the lower crossover: he will then return to set the wagons back on to the front of his train.

84 The afternoon pick up goods train re-assembled draws forward behind the North Box along the "crow" to continue to Boston, regaining the up main line by means of Station Box crossover No. 42. The engine is B1 No. 61159. The shunter (or perhaps it is the North signalman), now that the goods has been dealt with, is walking back across the tracks to resume whatever job he was doing before it arrived.

CHAPTER 8

SKEGNESS IS SO BRACING

"Skegness is so bracing": thus proclaimed the slogan on what is perhaps the most famous railway poster of all, John Hassall's "Jolly Fisherman", purchased by the Great Northern Railway in 1908 for £12. That doesn't sound much today, but it probably represented quite a few weeks pay for many railwaymen then. But the fame of the Lincolnshire coast was known long before that. For in 1845 in a prospectus for a direct railway from Lincoln to the coast we find a reference to "Skegness, that old and celebrated watering place near Wainfleet". Always with an eye open for business, the GNR from its early days promoted Skegness and Mablethorpe, offering reduced fare bookings to Burgh and Alford, where "conveyances" could be hired to complete the journey. The attractions of the Lincolnshire coast were such that before long the "conveyances" found themselves unable to cope with the traffic. The opening of the line to Skegness in 1873, and to Mablethorpe some years later, was doubtless welcomed alike by the resorts and the holidaymakers, and so the growth of the holiday traffic continued. The summer of 1878 found the GNR bringing nearly 76,000 people to Skegness, and two years later it was over 106,000. The difficulty for the railway was that virtually all the holiday trains approached from the south and therefore had to reverse at Firsby in order to gain the Skegness line. The inconvenience of this brought the GNR in 1874, only a year after the opening to Skegness, to obtain Parliamentary powers to build Firsby south curve. But it was not until 1881 that the work was completed, and on 29 May of that year a letter of approval was received from the Board of Trade just in time for the peak summer traffic. The curve was double track from the outset, even though the Skegness line was still single, and it proved its worth the following year when on August Bank Holiday 20,000 trippers came to Skegness by train. On that day the GNR used every available passenger coach and had to turn away two requests for special trains for lack of stock. It seems that the organisation of the return journeys was somewhat lacking, however, for one gathers that there were serious delays and some trains were up to 6 hours late! There must have been quite a procession of trains, - a spectacle to become familiar at Firsby for the next 85 years or so, reaching its peak in the decade up to 1939. A spectacle which I well remember watching, the evening trains viewed from our bedroom window looking across the fields to the triangle layout, at an hour when all good children should have been asleep (and my parents thought I was!). There was one occasion when the ghost of the 1882 gremlin must have been abroad, for late in the evening there were return trips held at all the signals round the curve and at the East, and there they waited. I believe there was trouble with a preceding train towards Little Steeping. Fortunately they were not 6 hours late but it was around midnight when the last train got on its way.

85 LNER class J6 No. 4276 bringing a trip for Skegness round the curve under the bridge at the East in 1947-8. These standard GNR general purpose engines were equally popular for passenger and goods, and in LNER days were frequently seen on excursions such as this. With its complement of Gresley coaches the train typifies the LNER.

86 A train from the London area on Saturday 4 August 1962. It is no less than the *Butlin Express* from Kings Cross, and is setting off round the curve as the signal has just cleared for him. The engine is 61179. The *Butlin Express* between Kings Cross and Skegness was a regular summer train in BR days, and was noted in the public time table as for Butlin's campers.

87 About two hours later that day the *Butlin Express* returns with its load of home-going campers. The special headboard was finished in Butlin's colours, blue lettering on a yellow ground.

Holiday trains approached Skegness and Mablethorpe from three directions - Boston, Lincoln, and Grimsby. Most trains from the Great Northern system, except those from the West Riding, came via Boston: from London and the south; Leicester (Belgrave Rd.) area; and the Derby Friargate route and its branches. Derby also provided access for LMS trains from the Birmingham, Stafford and Burton-on-Trent areas, while trains from Kettering and Northampton used the Nene valley line to Peterborough. All these trains travelled along the East Lincolnshire line from Boston to Firsby South. Via Lincoln came the GNR West Riding trains, and trains from the LMS Knottingley and Pontefract line; the Manchester and Sheffield areas of the GCR sent trains through Retford; and finally along the former Lancashire, Derbyshire & East Coast Railway came trains from Chesterfield and from GCR and Midland stations in Nottinghamshire. All trains via Lincoln used the New Line to Bellwater Junction and thence to Firsby South. These two routes - Lincoln and Boston - accounted for nine-tenths or more of the holiday traffic, the volume of which certainly justified Firsby south curve and kept the signalman in the South Box busy.

88 A junction with the Nottingham line at Bottesford gave access to the GN/LNW joint line and Leicester Belgrave Road. On Saturday 4 August 1962 B1 No. 61227 makes its way past the South Box, its train trailing round the curve. Leaving Skegness at 1-18 pm it is returning to Leicester Belgrave Road. The South down home signal towers in the foreground.

89 LNER K2 No. 1731 returning from Skegness in the summer of 1947. A Boston engine, so its destination is not known, perhaps Peterborough or Grantham.

90 There were many excursions from the Nottingham area, and here is excursion No. 489 checked as it draws up to the East down starter (Station Box No. 12) with Colwick engine 1732 of class K2. With the return to peace the LNER announced that *all* their engines would be painted in green passenger livery, but sadly the LNER ceased to exist before much progress could be made. No. 1732 received its LNER green at Cowlairs works in October 1947: this picture shows it in the early summer of 1948, one of the last examples of LNER splendour, and, like fig 85, a good example of an LNER train.

91. The 8-55 from Derby Friargate in charge of 61299 coming past the East home signal (Station box No. 11) on Saturday 1 August 1964. The tender is on the level crossing with the original village road. The opening of the south curve introduced this crossing within 100 yards of the first one across the line from the station. Eventually the East bridge, which appears in many of our pictures, was built and the road diverted. This crossing remained as an occupation crossing for access to the fields within the triangle.

92 Not for nothing was Skegness often referred to as Nottingham-on-Sea, for the GNR lines from Nottinghamshire and Derbyshire became the busiest of the routes to the Lincolnshire coast. A daily train to Skegness from Derby Friargate in the summer was almost a tradition, a Mablethorpe portion being detached at Boston and worked forward separately. But during August Mablethorpe had its own train from Nottingham. Here we see K3 No. 61826 bringing the Derby-Skegness train round the curve at the South on Saturday 4 August 1962, - one of its last duties, for it was withdrawn the next month.

93 The GNR route into Staffordshire via Derby Friargate provided access for LMS trains from the Midlands through Burton-on-Trent, and here is one of them. Taken from the lineside near the occupation crossing on the curve we see coming round under the East bridge 61285 of Colwick with train 1M41, the 2-39 from Skegness to Kings Norton on Saturday August 1 1964. (See also fig 21).

94 With the South Box framed in the bracket of the down home signal we see the driver looking forward at the cab window of K3 No. 61977 hauling the summer Saturday train from Derby Friargate at about 1-45 pm on 4 August 1962. A shot I like, but tinged with sadness, for this was another of my favourite K3s to be withdrawn in September.

95 The GNR Derby route also gave access via Egginton to the North Staffordshire line, and here a North Staffordshire excursion from Kidsgrove is coming round the curve at Firsby South on its way to Skegness on Saturday 1 August 1964 with B1 No. 61250 in charge.

96 Another train from the Midlands, on the morning of Bank Holiday 3 August 1964, from Burton-on-Trent itself this time. Train 1X26 is in charge of Colwick engine 61299, pulling away well at the East down starter after the slowing round the curve. The diamond sign on the signal post signifies that the line is track-circuited, and absolves the enginemen from the provisions of Rule 55, should they be brought to a stand.

Only two or three trains came through Grimsby; these were from places such as Leeds or Bradford which by taking this route could avoid Doncaster, an important consideration particularly during the busy years of the LNER. However, because they arrived at Firsby from the north, they had to reverse over one of the crossovers, which for this direction of movement were intended solely for shunting movements, and so the points actually facing the train as it set back had no facing point lock. I recall that over a period of many years these trains cheerfully set back over the unlocked points with no mishap at all, and I seem to remember that it was the top crossover from the up main to the Skegness line (No. 27) that was used. It would be locked at what was for this movement its trailing end by the combined facing point lock (No. 28) which it shared with that end of the through road. This offered complete protection, but not until the rear coach of the reversing train had reached the Skegness line. Then one day I arrived at the station to find tests in progress to scotch or clamp the points. Perhaps an instruction had been issued as a result of a mishap elsewhere. The scotch was easier and quicker to use but did not always secure the points firmly enough, and so it was the clamp that was used even though it was more fiddly. The result of this new practice was that trains were always set back over No 32 main crossover, as it was not so far to walk for the man with the clamp. But everyone apparently overlooked the fact that in reversing over the main crossover all of the train except the last coach would traverse the unlocked end of No. 27 crossover! I was told that more than once facing points from the up line to the Skegness line from the north had been asked for and refused. The reason given was that the curve was too sharp, but it was not so sharp as the south curve, and the real reason I think was the difficulty of sighting the necessary splitting signal, and the consequent risk of a mishap. There was no problem for returning trains, as there was direct access from the single line to the down main line via the through road and main crossover, locked and signalled for passenger train running.

97 A trip returning from Skegness in the summer or 1947, hauled by an ex-GCR 4-6-0 of LNER class B7, often called the 'Black Pigs'! [I recall seeing engines of this class on Eason's trips to London in the 1920s]. The train in the picture is most likely returning to Sheffield or Manchester, as at that time all the B7s were based at either Darnall or Gorton. In the distance behind the train the 4-arm South down home lattice bracket, still resplendant with its finials, can be seen.

98 Train 1E12, a relief train from Bradford Exchange, comes round from Firsby station to the East junction for Skegness at about 11-35 am on Saturday 1 August 1964. The engine is 61232 of Immingham. By travelling from Wakefield to Scunthorpe and Grimsby the train was able to use the Adwick Junction to Stainforth line to avoid the conjestion of Doncaster, a route used more frequently by the LNER than by BR.

99 The returning Bradford relief train later on Saturday 1 August 1964 coming from the East to the station, entering the single line section at No. 8 electric points, the electric motor machine for which can be clearly seen. Returning home the train was able to travel direct from the single line to the down main line for Grimsby without reversing. Again, as for fig 79, the photographer was on the site of the original Skegness branch level crossing. The south curve is in the background, the East home signal can just be seen behind the engine, and the second level crossing which appears in fig 91 is just out of sight by the hedge at the right hand edge of the picture.

100 The old GN/GE joint line via Gainsborough and Lincoln provided the route to the coast for trains from the West Riding, and here we see a Bradford to Skegness train approaching No. 57 crossing on Saturday 4 August 1962 with 61110 in charge. An early start for the holiday-makers,- having left Bradford at 7-48 am.

101 Following the New Line to Lincoln and the former GCR route to Retford the 4-2 pm daily summer train from Skegness to Sheffield Victoria comes round the curve to the South on Wednesday 31 July 1963. For some strange reason the engine - 61374 - is displaying the stopping train headlamp code.

102 It is almost 8 o'clock in the evening of Wednesday 24 July 1964 as ex-LMS 44851 passes the East up home signal hauling a return excursion for Trowell, Pye Bridge, and other stations on the former Midland Nottingham & Sheffield line, using the LDEC route from Lincoln to Shirebrook. The use of LM region (ex-LMS) engines is an echo of the occasional incidence of an LMS engine working through to Skegness on a day trip in LNER days.

103 In the sunshine of Saturday 31 August 1963 ex-LMS 4-6-0 No. 44861 pulls away from the South with the 2 pm from Skegness for Radford, its train still trailing round the curve. This train travelled via Lincoln along the old Lancashire, Derbyshire & East Coast Railway towards Chesterfield as far as Shirebrook and thence the Midland line through Kirkby-in-Ashfield. I wonder for what pilot duty the engine was prepared on the previous Wednesday as directed by the chalked notice on the front buffer-beam?

The diversity of starting points for the excursion traffic resulted in a corresponding variety of coaching stock used. Naturally those of Great Northern and LNER origin predominated, 6-wheeler as well as bogie vehicles, with other constituents of the LNER well represented also. And the occasional train of LMS maroon seemed completely foreign to our youthful eyes; little did we dream that in a couple of decades or so we would be seeing all coaches sporting that colour. As the years passd the older pre-grouping vehicles were seen less frequently, particularly after nationalization when large numbers of BR standard mark 1 coaches were built. However, the transfer of the former LNER lines in the Nottingham area to the LM region temporarily increased the numbers of former LMS coaches on the Skegness excursions from that area. But at the August Bank Holiday peak period in the 1930s almost anything that would run on wheels could be pressed into service. An interesting example of this was the frequent use of sets of London suburban coaches for weekend excursions, their destination blinds bearing their weekday station, names strange to us, such as New Barnet and Gordon Hill. The use of these sets was not confined to excursions from London: many were worked empty at the weekend to provincial stations, usually in the East Midlands, and after their jaunt to Skegness returned to London overnight. This practice was continued by BR until the coaches were scrapped as diesel or electric trains took over the London suburban services.

Peak summer weekends were busy in those days. The Saturday service in August would include over 40 trains round the curve, half a dozen trains for Skegness which came via Grimsby, 15-18 trains for Mablethorpe, and perhaps another half dozen which combined or divided in Firsby station; then there

104 Standing at the South down home signal on Saturday 4 August 1962 is a train from the far end of the old Manchester, Sheffield & Lincolnshire Railway, in charge of 61177. Leaving Manchester Central at 8-10 am it came over the Pennines to Sheffield Victoria, thence via Retford to reach the GNR at Lincoln and at 12-20 it is checked while the train seen retreating in the distance goes past on the up line.

were the daily 'main line' trains and the Skegness & Lincoln New Line service; the local service; and of course the goods and fish trains. Add to these scheduled trains the holiday relief portions and a goodly number of excursions, and there would be well over 150 trains handled by Firsby Boxes in the day. Indeed the LNER said as much in a press release in the 1930s, when additional sidings were built at Skegness because Skegness alone dealt with more than 100 trains a day in the peak season. On such occasions the stretch of line between Bellwater Junction and Firsby South could well have been one of the busiest in the country. Sundays and August Bank Holiday were just about as busy for day trips came to Skegness from all over the place: almost anywhere and everywhere on the old GN & GC systems, but also quite a few LMS trains would be seen. On rare occasions a LMS engine would work right through to Skegness. Of course all these trips arrived at the coast during the morning, and did not set off for home until the evening. During the afternoon, because of the inadequacy of Skegness turntable, strings of engines coupled together would make the 20 mile round trip to Firsby and back to turn on the triangle; there would also be some from Mablethorpe and for them it was a 30 mile jaunt! Not only that but Skegness sidings usually overflowed, and many trains came to Firsby for storage for the afternoon, in the North sidings, but especially along the Spilsby line: the rake of trains would often extend as far as Great Steeping or even further. It was on the Spilsby line that I had my first close look at an LMS engine, an 0-6-0, for our route to and from Sunday School was the public footpath across the line, and one day there it was, right by the footpath, with its train and crew.

A curious mishap befell one of these day trips sometime between 1928 and 1932. The rear wheelset of the rear bogie of the rear coach (the last pair of wheels of the train) became derailed at the East spring points, and fell to the right of the track. The train stopped with the derailed wheels just past the occupation crossing near the bridge. The rear coach was detached and the train went on its way. I well remember stopping on the way home from Sunday School to watch the re-railing. The coach was kept in a siding at Firsby for a long while; meantime it, the track, and any other relevant equipment were thoroughly examined but nothing was found to account for the mishap, which as far as I am aware is still unexplained. There appears to be no reference in official records; there being no injury or damage perhaps no official report was called for. But in the late 1930s one of Firsby staff put forward to me the theory that the last wheels (more probably in fact the last bogie) of the rear coach failed to operate track circuits, and so as soon as the front bogie of that coach cleared the spring points it would release the track circuit and hence release conflicting levers. It was suggested that the signal was promptly put up behind the train and a move made to pull No. 8 points for the next local train from Skegness, but by mistake No. 9 (set back disc) was pulled. A small movement of that lever would detect the spring points normal, and it might have been possible to have done this in time to catch that last wheelset causing it to derail to the right! Though fitting the facts, it is only a theory and cannot be proved.

Those summers were certainly Firsby's busiest times; after 1945 things were never quite the same. The railways did make valient efforts amid the turmoil of nationalization to recover from the burden of war, and holiday traffic began to revive. By the mid 1950s there were once more 40 or more scheduled workings round the curve on a peak summer Saturday and there were still almost as many in 1963. But over the next two years while the first closure proposals - which included Skegness - were contested the schedule had fallen to 30 workings. To and from Mablethorpe there were 16 workings on peak Saturdays up to 1963; two years later there were only eight. But post-1945 excursion traffic never approached the volume of former years, and there was never any question of the sidings at Skegness overflowing. Doubtless road competition, aided by the end of petrol rationing, and coupled with the increase in paid annual holidays, encouraged the decline, until by 1964 the most popular day out - August Bank Holiday - saw a mere dozen or so trips to Skegness and five to Mablethorpe. There is no doubt that Firsby owes much to its status as a junction and to the Skegness traffic. I was fortunate to be able to record some of the activity in the years after 1946, and though of course the ubiquitous B1 engines tend to monopolise the pictures, an attempt has been made to include some varied viewpoints, and examples of trains from many different places. Over the more recent history of the Skegness traffic it is perhaps best to draw a veil.

105 On Saturday 4 August 1962 the 11-27 from Mablethorpe to Basford casts a cloud over the South Box as it dashes past in the morning sunshine.

106 On Saturday 31 August 1963 61264 bowls merrily past the South up home signal with the 12-56 from Mablethorpe for Derby Friargate. After withdrawal this engine spent some time as a stationary boiler prior to purchase for restoration by the Thompson B1 Locomotive Trust.

107 The Hughes class 5 'Crab' 2-6-0 was a type of engine not often seen in Lincolnshire, but was rostered for this turn in 1963. Former LMS 42799 is in charge of the 6-40 am from Radford at No. 67 crossing on its way to Mablethorpe on Saturday 31 August, having come by way of Shirebrook West and the LDEC line.

108 A view from the top of the South Box steps, showing both the up main and up branch home signals of the South, as 61390 hurries along with the 12-5 from Mablethorpe to Nottingham Victoria on Saturday 1 August 1964. In the background can be seen the line of mineral wagons stored on the stub end of all that remains of the Spilsby line.

109 The 9-20 SX peak summer train from Nottingham Victoria dashes past the South Box on its way to Mablethorpe on Friday 31 July 1964 with 61361 in charge. In the early and late season this train is combined with the Derby-Skegness train, the two halves dividing at Boston.

110 On Satuday 1 August 1964 43087 has come from Boston to take charge of the Skegness portion of the 6-38 am from Radford, a combined Mablethorpe and Skegness train which divides in Firsby station. Having been round via the East to turn, it is here seen coming across the through road to the down platform, from whence it will go on to the Spilsby line to await the train.

111 The enginemen from Boston in charge of 43087, prior to their taking out the Skegness portion of the Radford train.

112 The 6-28 am from Radford, via the LDEC line and New Line, has arrived and the front part has left for Mablethorpe. The rear portion is leaving for Skegness with the engine on the through road to the Skegness line. The division at Firsby of trains such as this which travelled via Lincoln and the New Line was a fairly frequent pre-war practice, but less so in BR days.

113 At the East at about 1 pm on 1 August 43087 brings the returning Skegness portion of the Radford train under the bridge and round the single line to the station to join the Mablethorpe return portion to form train 1E30. Through the bridge the home signal can be seen, the arm for the route to the station at clear.

114 Three quarters of an hour later 43087, its task completed, sets off light engine for Boston past the South up main home signal.

CHAPTER 9

DAYS IN THE LIFE OF FIRSBY STATION

Enough has been said already of the different train services at Firsby for it to be apparent that operations at this country junction could at times be quite complex. In this chapter an attempt will be made to show how the various services fitted together into an operating day, and, through some detailed sequences, to see what the working life of the station and signalboxes was like at different times. In following these descriptive sequences the plan of the station and track (fig 8) and the fold-out signalling plan (fig 138) will be found useful.

The most simply-organised of the services at Firsby, the one that most nearly fitted the pattern of the 'typical' country junction was the Spilsby branch. The 'one engine in steam' was kept at Spilsby, and ran its couple of coaches up and down to Firsby, - even the goods was completely local. But there was an occasion when I remember a railmotor was tried out on the Spilsby line for a short while in LNER days, probably around 1930. At that time I knew little about railmotors: this was the only time that I have seen one in action, and I did not get a chance to travel in it. From my recollection of it I feel sure that it would have been one of the Sentinel cars, of which the LNER had a fair number, and its short stay was probably because its use precluded the running of mixed trains. Skegness, though, was somewhat different. There was indeed a local branch train, with the engine kept at Wainfleet, the original terminus of the line. This train was four or five coaches, longer in the summer: no mixed trains or railmotors on the Skegness line. But there were also one or two through trains to and from Skegness, which called at Firsby except when the South was open in the summer. And Firsby was effectively the junction for the New Line service. All trains on the New Line were through services between Skegness and Lincoln (sometimes Retford or Sheffield), and all - save the odd one on a summer Saturday - called at Firsby. Quite often, too,

there would be, again especially in summer, a local train from Mablethorpe to Firsby and back in the morning and evening to avoid stopping the Cleethorpes and London express at Willoughby.

And we must not forget the mail and parcels. Besides the local parcels business Firsby was the junction for this traffic as well as for passengers, and transfer between trains caused considerable activity (figs 115 & 116). Quite a number of barrows were kept at Firsby for this purpose, and the staff doubtless kept fit heaving them across the tracks between platforms. Quite an effort: two or often three man-power was required to haul a loaded barrow up the platform end ramps. Going down the ramps the staff became expert at riding a 4-wheeler, steering it by an outstretched hand on the handle. Not a little skill was required - particularly when descending the down side ramp, for at the foot of this one there was a sharp left turn due to the acute angle of the level crossing. Traditionally parcels were dispatched by the next available passenger train, but when the East Lincolnshire line services became two-car diesel units with small brake compartments it was found necessary to run special loco-hauled parcels trains (fig 117).

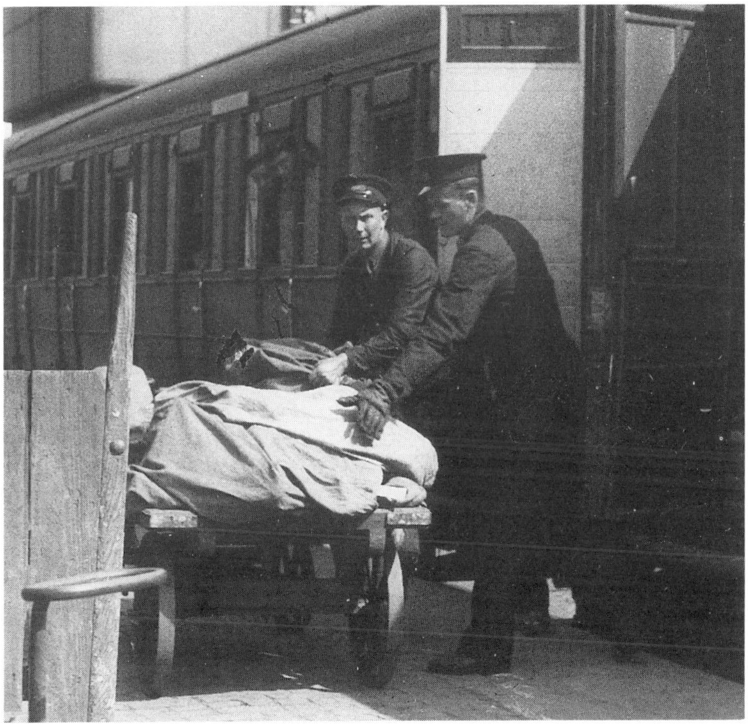

116 Mails being loaded on the Skegness train on a sunny morning in the last months of the LNER. The small roofboard of the branch train was lettered *Skegness.* A couple of passengers seem intent on the photographic activity! Facing the camera is Mr. Dickson, another long-serving member of Firsby staff; assisting him is Mr. D. Duncan.

115 (opposite) Long-serving member of Firsby staff, Mr. Penson (left), supervises the loading of parcels on a train at the Skegness platform on a sunny afternoon in the autumn of 1946. Facing the camera is Mr. K. Smith, and with his back to the camera is Mr. Ginlee.

117 Traditionally parcels were dispatched by the next available passenger train, but the increasing use for passenger services of diesel units with restricted brake compartment space resulted in the appearance of separate parcels trains. Here one is seen in the afternoon sunshine of Thursday 19 August 1963 ambling past the North Box to its stop in the station.

There was one two-wheel barrow equipped with a large wicker basket secifically for handling mails (figs 118 & 119). Indeed, especially after the suspension of the Spilsby passenger service, the Post Office arranged certain postmen's rounds to include a spell at Firsby assisting with the mail transfer, for though mailbags would travel on almost any train, there were certain busier times of day. A mountain of mail and newspapers for local delivery arrived from Peterborough at 4-30 am on the train run primarily for that purpose, while the main outgoing mail was dispatched on the up mail train to Peterborough at 9 pm, a large amount of it arriving at 8-40 pm on the train from Skegness. There being no service on the Spilsby line after 7 pm, Spilsby Post Office sent their large van load of mails to arrive at Firsby at 8-35 pm. On his way down the postman emptied the roadside posting boxes at Halton and Great Steeping, and finally the one on Firsby station, giving the villages the luxury of a 8-15 to 8-30 "last collection". Unfranked and unsorted, the letters were put in a special mailbag which was secured by a padlock after the final collection at Firsby, before being dispatched on the train to Peterborough. The letters received a *Peterborough, Northants* cancellation, to the confusion of the addressees! The special bag 'returned empty' at 4-30 am the next day. Needless to say this happens no more!

All in all then, there were some interesting operations at Firsby. The working day began early with the 4-30 am down mail and newspaper train. Next came the Boston to Skegness goods, which kept the North yard busy for a while, and left for Skegness before the arrival of the first branch passenger train from there to meet the 7 o'clock up stopping train. At 8 o'clock came the up *Flying Flea,* then the 8-30 down stopping train, and the first of the Skegness to Lincoln through trains. These through trains between Lincoln and Skegness had to reverse at Firsby, which required the engine to run round to the other end of the train, a fairly simple process taking a few minutes and earning the signalman a few extra marks. One of the advantages claimed for the multiple unit diesel trains introduced by BR was the saving from the elimination of engine movements such as these. Quite so, but the diesel cars were also required to be capable of hauling the van of fish, or other perishable goods, regularly attached to passenger trains. And so, at Firsby in the 1950s, we had the interesting spectacle of the complete diesel train running round one van! Then at 10 am the morning Cleethorpes to London express called, the start of a fairly steady series of four or five trains up and down the main line, two or three between Lincoln and Skegness, through goods trains each way, and around mid-day the pick up goods from Lincoln arrived; ending with

118 Mails transfer between trains as part of postal duties: two postmen load mail on the mid-day Skegness to Lincoln train on 17 June 1954. About to open the brake compartment door is my late father, who joined the Post Office as temporary war-time helper and was still working for them ten years after the war ended! The 'Gentlemen' sign is of cast metal letters screwed to a timber base, the whole surrounded by a timber frame with an inner moulding. Notices at Firsby were of this form, or a single iron casting (figs 73 & 119), but were changed within the next couple of years to BR blue & white sheet metal signs. The train is made up of Gresley teak coaches in the early BR red and cream livery.

the afternoon Grimsby to Peterborough express with through London coaches calling a little before 2 pm. For the next couple of hours the station itself was quiet, but not so the North. For besides through goods trains each way and empty fish trains returning to Grimsby, there was a pick up goods in each direction, the Lincoln goods was dispatched on its return journey, and the Spilsby goods arrived, shunted in the yard, and returned to Spilsby. After this burst of goods activity there followed a sequence of passenger trains, one up and one down between 4 and 4-30 pm, an up stopping train just after 6 pm, at 7 pm the returning London to Cleethorpes express, and the last Lincoln to Skegness through train of the day. Again there followed one of the quiet intervals for a couple of hours, but during that time, just after 7 pm and at about 8 pm, the two express fish trains from Grimsby to London ran through. Then at 9 pm came a down stopping train and the up mail train, followed at 9-45 pm by the day's final passenger

119 An early 1948 photograph of my late father with the postal barrow on mail transfer duty at Firsby. Of interest is the warning notice, this one a metal casting with raised letters; by 1957 it had been replaced by a blue and white BR sign with different wording (fig 16).

train, the returning *Flying Flea* for Grimsby. All passenger trains on the main line except the 4-30 am down mail had a Skegness connection - either the branch train or a through train between Skegness and Lincoln; while the Spilsby train met all trains from the 8-30 am down stopping train to the 7 pm London to Cleethorpes express. To round off the day the up 'midnight goods' ran through at about 10-30 pm and finally a light engine returned from Skegness to Boston; then at last about 11 pm the late shift signalman could close the Box and go home.

While the basic pattern of services changed little over a period of many years, the times of some individual trains could vary widely with each re-issue of the timetable. It was the late morning trains which were most affected, especially in summer when holiday services had to be fitted into the schedule. But there were certain trains the timing of which remained more or less constant. Examples were the London expresses, the early morning trains, and of course the mail trains: the evening Grimsby to Peterborough mail in particular having run to the same timings since the middle of the nineteenth century.

It was not often that Firsby was the first to see something new, but I remember one such occasion in the summer of 1933. In that year the LNER built some special tourist trains, each comprising 12 coaches including two buffet cars. They were completely open plan, with light modern interiors, and finished externally in cream above and locomotive green below the waistline. The first booked run started from a Lincolnshire station, and so after being shown to the top brass at Kings Cross in late July the first train set appeared at Firsby and was parked all Sunday in the Skegness bay platform line. I can clearly remember being given a conducted tour of the train. I remember it looking very smart indeed. After 1939 the vehicles were used in ordinary service on various parts of the LNER system including the East Lincolnshire line. I recall travelling in one on the Sunday evening Grimsby to Kings Cross train when returning from war-time leave. The buffet cars lasted into the 1960s, and I was able to make use of the service of one or two of them before their withdrawal.

In the following paragraphs an attempt is made to describe in more detail some typical sequences of work, all from my own observations. Two sequences are described from the viewpoint of the signalbox, and mention some details of the operation of the block system, a method of working which is rapidly being displaced from regular railway use; the other sequence describes the arrival and departure of the morning express from Cleethorpes and the connecting services, and provides an observer's view of the working of the station itself.

120 The return Skegness goods at Firsby East on Thursday 30 July 1964, with signals clear for him to go round to the South and on to Little Steeping. There being no calls to pay on the return journey to Boston the unfitted through goods headcode is displayed. The engine is 43081, one of the 2-6-0 engines of the former LMS which were designed by H. G. Ivatt, son of H. A. Ivatt whose famous Atlantics hauled the expresses through Firsby in the 1930s (fig 1). A number of these 2-6-0s were based at Boston in BR days and were used on all sorts of jobs.

Our first sequence is set in the South Box in 1937, when - as mentioned in chapter 7 - it was opened each afternoon for a short while to allow the returning Skegness goods to travel direct round the curve on its way to Boston. It is summer, and we join Relief Signalman Bullock of Ropsley as he arrives at the Box. On "switching in" we note with satisfaction that the instruments remain at LINE BLOCKED; we signal the opening code (5-5-5) to the station and Little Steeping, and put up the main line signals which are left at clear when the Box is closed. We have not many minutes to wait before the goods is offered from the East; we accept it and set the points (No. 13). No sooner done than Little Steeping offers the 3-57 down passenger train, so these two trains will arrive at about the same time, which today is unfortunate, for the goods engine has to go to the station for water. So the passenger train is accepted up to the home signal only by returning "13 bells" (3-5-5), that is "section clear but junction blocked". In the ordinary way a passenger train would be given precedence, but to do so in this instance will mean the goods engine remaining here until the 4-22 up passenger train has passed. So the decision is made to send the goods engine to the station first, so that he can take water while the down passenger is at the platform, and be back here at the South before the up train arrives.

A couple of minutes go by and almost simultaneously Little Steeping signals TRAIN ON LINE for the 3-57 down, and the East (Station) signals TRAIN ON LINE for the goods. The goods comes slowly round the curve and as it comes to a halt the home signal (19) is pulled off. The fireman jumps down, pins the brakes on the leading wagons, uncouples, and the engine draws forward past the Box as we offer it to the Station. The down passenger is now approaching: we wait until it has stopped at the down home signal before setting the crossover and clearing No. 8 disc. The engine sets off and TRAIN ON LINE is signalled to the Station while the clean green Atlantic waits with the passenger train. No. 8 disc and the crossover are restored. Soon the goods engine is clear, the Station rings OUT OF SECTION, and the passenger train is offered and accepted. The down signals (Nos. 2 & 3) are cleared, and ON LINE signalled to the Station. As the down train passes the down home (2) is put up. A couple of minutes elapse, OUT OF SECTION is received from the Station, No. 3 is put up, and OUT OF SECTION passed on to Little Steeping.

Next the Station offers the 4-2 pm Lincoln train: it is offered to Little Steeping straightaway. The up main line signals are cleared (16, 17, 18). Very soon the Station signals TRAIN ON LINE which is passed on to Little Steeping. As the train goes on his way the signals are put up behind him, and OUT OF SECTION signalled to the Station. Before very long the Station offers the goods engine; the up main home (17) is cleared, TRAIN ON LINE rings from the Station, and the engine trundles up alongside clear of the junction points. No. 17 is restored, the points (No. 13) reversed, and the engine sets back to his train on the curve. There are still ten minutes or more before the up passenger is due, so it is decided to get the goods on its way. The home signal on the curve

121 LNER 1082 hauling Gresley coaches at No. 57 crossing in 1947. A down stopping train,- almost certainly the 4 pm, which in the 1930s was a New England GNR Atlantic turn, but now has an Immingham B1. The bogie passenger van next to the engine will be noted in addition to the luggage space in the second vehicle. It was the lack of this sort of accommodation in the diesel units that resulted in the running of separate parcels trains.

122 Lincoln engine LNER 2915, another of the ex-GCR 'Jersey Lillies', approaching No. 57 crossing at the South with a Skegness-Lincoln train in 1947. The through trains between Lincoln and Skegness formed the basic service of the New Line for the whole of its 57 year existence.

123 The 4-22 pm up local train at Firsby station in 1936, with Robinson 4-4-0 No. 6030 in charge. This was one of the jobs over the East Lincolnshire line allotted to Immingham engines and men after the LNER came into being. On this turn the engine worked the the 4-22 up local shown here to Boston, where it took over from a New England Atlantic the returning London-Cleethorpes express calling at Firsby at 7 pm. I well remember this box camera photograph, for it was taken at the request of the enginemen: I was directed down on to the track to take it, and I am happy to add that they were pleased with the results on receiving the prints when next on this turn.

(No. 19) is cleared for him to come forward to the advance signal (No. 16) which he does as soon as he has coupled up and unpinned the brakes. As he approaches the advance signal we hear OUT OF SECTION from Little Steeping for the Lincoln so the goods is offered and the advance signal cleared. The goods gives a blast on the whistle and sets off as TRAIN ON LINE is sent to Little Steeping, and the home signal and points are restored. As the goods gets on his way No. 16 is put up and OUT OF SECTION signalled to the Station and also to the East.

A couple of minutes or so elapses and then the up passenger due in the station at 4-15 is offered, which means it has left Burgh. About five minutes later the goods reaches Little Steeping so the up passenger, which has arrived in the station, is offered and the main line signals cleared (16, 17, 18). Prompt on time TRAIN ON LINE is received from the Station for the 4-22 up; this is an Immingham D9 turn to Boston: he will return with the express due at Firsby at 7 pm (fig 123). TRAIN ON LINE is signalled to Little Steeping, and as the train passes the signals are put up, and OUT OF SECTION signalled to the Station. Eventually OUT OF SECTION is received from Little Steeping, all lines are now clear and the box may be closed. To Little Steeping and the Station the code 5-5-7 is signalled: both respond with a LINE CLEAR peg, allowing our main line signals (1, 2, 3, 16, 17, 18) to be pulled off. This done a single stroke on the bell in each direction and both reply with the 5-5-7 code. The block switch is turned from IN to OUT, the train register entry made, the Box is locked up and we return to the station.

A year or two have rolled by as we wander along to the station on a summer morning to see one of our favourite GNR Atlantics call with the London express, and to observe the various connecting services. We arrive at the station as the gates are closing, and the 9-58 all stations from Mablethorpe runs in at the up platform, a rake of ex-GNR coaches with one of the ex-GNR C12 4-4-2 tank engines (fig 124). The engine uncouples and runs forward to the top crossover (No. 27). This is reversed, and he runs back through the bay platform line to the north end water crane to spend the next two or three minutes filling his tanks. Meantime the gates are opened: there is quite a bit of traffic about in the summer.

Having taken water the engine goes forward towards the North Box and gives a crow on the whistle. No. 41 crossover and No. 42 disc are reversed and he comes back to his train. Coupled up, the train returns along the 'crow' line to the up sidings to await departure in half an hour's time.

As he does so two shrieks of a whistle are heard from the direction of Barton's crossing, the platform bell rings twice, the gates close again, and the Spilsby train runs in at the down platform. Another C12 tank - probably 4504 or 4537 - with its two ex-GNR flat-sided coaches, a six-wheeler brake third weighing fourteen and a half tons and a bogie brake composite of twentytwo and a half tons. He runs right up to the end of the platform where he, too, takes water. The handful of passengers alight and there are a few parcels to unload. The down inner home signal at the platform end, No. 17, is pulled off

124 The local train from Mablethorpe arriving in 1947. The well-remembered flat-sided coaches, with the guard's compartment ducket, hauled by C12 tank engine No. 7374 (old 4519) make up a typical GNR train a quarter of a century after grouping and almost at the end of the existence of the LNER. A Louth engine and men. The engine was transferred to the London area in January 1948. (This picture is in fact the evening working to meet the returning down express.)

for him to go to the North to run round his train, and perhaps sort a few wagons. As he leaves one of the yard staff jumps aboard to open the North Box.

Now everything seems to happen at once! Three blasts of a whistle are heard from the East echoed by three rings on the platform bell. No. 6 signal on the bracket by the single line changes to clear, and the local train from Skegness, with a D3 4-4-0, runs in alongside the bay platform, to shouts of *Firsby, All Change*. At the same time it seems, the up main line signals are cleared and four rings sound on the platform bell. Looking northward we see a white cloud of steam as the express makes its way from Burgh, and as he approaches the station the Skegness local draws out of the bay platform line forward into the 'crow' to make way for the Skegness-Lincoln through train.

The express is a long train and it stops with the front part by the platform and the clean green Atlantic by the platform end. This is a stroke of luck for we now have a chance to observe it while above the steady din of carriage doors and people chattering the station staff shout forth -- *Firsby! Firsby! Change for Skegness and Spilsby! Boston, Spalding, Peterborough, and London! Through the Archway Lincoln! Over the bridge Skegness and Spilsby!* Gradually the hubbub subsides, whistles sound and the train draws forward to bring the rear half to the platform. As the coaches pass we note the roofboards with bold letters *Kings Cross Grimsby and Cleethorpes.* I remember on one occasion seeing a roofboard inscribed *London (Kings +) Grimsby and Cleethorpes.* More shouts, whistles and arm waving bring the train to a halt. Yet again the staff shout their directions for the passengers, and now to the slamming of doors is added the sound of barrows trundled along and the noise of mails and parcels being loaded and unloaded.

Looking to the North we see the Spilsby train in the siding alongside the goods shed. While we have been paying our respects to the Ivatt Atlantic the Spilsby engine has run round its coaches using the down siding crossovers at the North, and has left the down line clear for the next train. At last the loading is complete and the New England Atlantic (which came down on the 4-30 am mail) sets off vigorously for Boston with the express. The platform bell rings three again, we see that the single line bracket signal, No. 6, is at clear, and alongside the bay platform runs the Skegness to Lincoln train to shouts of *Lincoln Train!* and *Over the bridge Spilsby and Mablethorpe!* from the staff. Barrows are trundled along for more parcel loading, meanwhile those for local delivery, Spilsby, and Skegness, are trundled across the line to the down platform. The gates are opened again, the long occupation by the express has caused a long line of traffic to collect.

125 A train arriving from Skegness in 1947. Tender-first running was quite common on the Skegness branch. The engine is 2908, one of the GCR Robinson Atlantics of LNER class C4, a number of which were sent to Lincolnshire after the war in place of GNR types. The staff on the crossing and platform are taking note of the photographer! Crossing the track is Mr. Carey; by the gatepost is Ken Smith, and the man in the distance on the platform could well be Mr. Greg Dickson.

126 LNER 1073 of class B1 running into the station in 1947 with the up 10 am Cleethorpes-London express. A new engine, built by the North British Locomotive Co. in September 1946. I remember this, of course, as a regular New England Ivatt Atlantic turn, but by this time there were few Atlantics left, while large numbers of new B1 engines were being delivered, and so they took over this, and other similar, duties.

Now coming from the North along the up line is the engine of the earlier arrival from Skegness, to take over the Lincoln train. He draws up to the inner home signal at the platform and waits while the gates are closed and it clears; he then runs forward to the Skegness line crossover. The signal goes up and as he comes to rest the crossover, No. 27, and disc, No. 26, are reversed. He sets back to the train at the bay platform; the disc is restored, but the crossover remains reversed for his departure, for which the lower arm (36) of the bay platform signal is pulled off. Meantime the engine that brought the train in from Skegness has uncoupled and will go forward to the crow to collect the local Skegness set due to depart in threequarters of an hour's time. The Lincoln train now departs.

The platform bell rings again and we notice that the down main home and inner home are at clear. Approaching is the Lincoln to Skegness train: it draws up at the down platform to shouts of *Wainfleet and Skegness! Change for Mablethorpe and Spilsby!* and the usual platform bustle. The signalman restores the home signal and takes the opportunity for a quick wind of the gates to let the road traffic get away. The engine uncouples and runs forward to the North and the inner home is restored. Returning over one of the crossovers there to the up line he, too, is checked by the up inner home while the gates close before going forward to return over the main crossover to his train (figs 128 & 129).

Once more many things seem to happen at once. Once the Lincoln-Skegness engine is clear of the North, the Mablethorpe train leaves the refuge of the up siding to the up line, and the Spilsby train leaves the down siding and draws towards the station on the down line. The Mablethorpe then crosses to the down line by the top crossover at the North. At the station the through road is set and the topmost arm (34) of the 3-arm signal is cleared. The train from Lincoln sets off for Skegness, and as he does so the Spilsby train creeps up behind him alongside the down platform. There are shouts of *Spilsby! Spilsby!* as the passengers and parcels board the train. Meantime, it being Wednesday, the MWSO Cleethorpes-Skegness train has arrived at the North and is held at the up main home. With the engine movements at the North completed and the up line clear, that signal may now be cleared for him to come into the station.

Quickly the through road is restored, the Spilsby points are set as the Spilsby driver goes over to the post beside the three-arm signal. He opens the hatch, inserts the train staff into the socket, turns it to the right, returns it and withdraws it. The needle moves from *locked* to *free,* and the lowest arm of the signal (23) is pulled off. The needle returns to *locked,* and the driver to his engine. A wave of the guard's flag, a toot on the whistle, and off he goes, and the signal returns to *danger.*

Now the Mablethorpe train sets back alongside the down platform to appropriate shouts from the staff, and the down line signals are cleared for his departure.

While all this has been going on the train from Cleethorpes has been drawn forward on the up line beyond the main crossover. The Mablethorpe train leaves. The main crossover is reversed, and one of the staff who went forward with the Cleethorpes train secures the crossover with the clamp kept there for the purpose: that end of the crossover has no facing point lock and so must be clamped for a passenger-carrying train to pass over it in that direction.

The disc - No. 31 - is cleared and the train sets back alongside the down platform, the clamp is removed, the through road is set, the upper arm of the 3-arm signal (34) is cleared and the train sets off for Skegness. The signal is restored and the gates opened once more.

The time is now 10-38, and there is a twenty minute gap before the Spilsby train returns to meet the next main line trains. Leaving the staff to book in the parcels for delivery we wend our way home. During the past 45 minutes the Station and North Boxes have between them dealt with four through trains, three requiring reversal, and three branch trains; also upwards of a dozen engine movements; while the station staff have been fully occupied directing a goodly crowd of passengers and handling parcels and mails.

127 The 10-30 am Lincoln-Skegness train in early 1948. The train has arrived at the down platform, water has been taken, and the fireman inches his way along the narrow footplating back to the cab. The inner home signal, almost hidden by the water crane, is pulled off for the engine to go forward to the North to run round. The water crane control valve handle seen in the picture was subsequently replaced by a handwheel, see fig 60.

128 Having crossed over to the up main line at the North, the engine of the Lincoln-Skegness train is seen as it runs back through the station preparatory to setting back on to the other end of its train. LNER 7442, class C14, is one of Robinson's second series of 4-4-2 tank engines for the GCR, and was allocated to Lincoln shed.

129 The engine is setting back on to the coaches ready to leave for Skegness. Standing in the six-foot in earnest conversation with someone on the platform is Mr. Penson as he waits for the engine to buffer up.

Our final sequence recounts from the viewpoint of the Station Box the events of Tuesday morning 4 August 1964, the day after Bank Holiday. It makes an interesting comparison with the earlier ones, for example the use of diesel cars has done away with the engine movements that formerly required the attention of the North Box. It also illustrates how, because it controls the East junction, the Station Box is involved in the working of the Skegness trains going round the curve.

It is about 10-45, as we greet Signalman Moore of Burgh : he has just accepted from Wainfleet the Skegness local train due at 11-1. On the Skegness branch Wainfleet is the only intermediate box switched in : this was usual except on busy days such as summer Saturdays and Bank Holidays. The South is open of course, an empty stock train has already gone round to Skegness and there are excursions to follow as well as the regular daily train from Derby. At about 10-50 TRAIN ON LINE is received as the local train leaves Wainfleet; about five minutes later it has called at Thorpe Culvert and is observed entering the approach track circuit A1. The motors are reversed (8, 7), and the East home signal (5) cleared. The gates are closed, the bay platform approach signal (6) pulled off, and three rings sounded on the platform bell to annonce the train's arrival. As he comes round on the single line No. 5 is put up and the motors restored. The train, a 'double set' - i.e. two twin-car diesel units - in anticipation of extra passengers, trundles in at the bay platform, No. 6 is put up, and OUT OF SECTION given to Wainfleet.

The gates are opened and the waiting traffic goes across. Wainfleet now offers 2-3, a light engine for Boston. The Skegness arrival is reported to Control, who tell us that the 11-9 down train was held up at Spalding; it is so badly overcrowded that a relief train has been sent ahead as far as Firsby. The South is called on the local phone circuit to tell him of the delays. Then Wainfleet signals TRAIN ON LINE for the light engine, it is offered round the curve to the South, and the East home signal (No. 2) pulled off.

Before very long the South offers the down relief train, which means that it has left Little Steeping. The gates are closed in readiness for it. Watching the progress of the light engine on the track diagram, once it is observed arriving at the East TRAIN ON LINE is signalled to the South, and when track A clears No. 2 is put up. A minute or so later the South signals it OUT OF SECTION, and OUT OF SECTION is passed on to Wainfleet.

Soon we receive TRAIN ON LINE for the down relief: the down home (16) is pulled off and the handgates locked. One ring on the platform bell announces its approach. The train - a two-car diesel - runs in 6 minutes after the scheduled train was due, and one wonders how the crowd that now throngs the platform managed to get in it! Most of the passengers go over the bridge to the Skegness train, but there are some who await the arrival of the scheduled train. No. 16 is put up and the gates are opened. The relief is offered back to the South as empty stock (ECS), to return to Boston, and the main crossover is set for it (32, 33). Traffic over the crossing is interrupted as the gates are closed (fig 50); No. 37 signal is pulled off and the handgates locked. The ECS diesel car hoots and leaves for Boston; the up starter (35) is pulled off and TRAIN ON LINE signalled to the South. No. 37 is put up and the crossover restored. The handgates are released. OUT OF SECTION is signalled to the South now that the relief no longer blocks the down line. The gates are opened again for the waiting road traffic (fig 49) and the up starter (35) put up behind the departing ECS.

Now the South offers the scheduled Peterborough-Grimsby train, and follows this with OUT OF SECTION for the ECS. The down train is offered to Burgh. We wait for the road traffic to get out of the way (why is it that immediately a train is in section cars appear as from nowhere to cross the line?). TRAIN ON LINE rings from the South, and at last the gates can be closed. Three signals are cleared for the train (it is too close for the distant) and the platform bell rung once to announce it; the home is put up as he runs in ten minutes late. No wonder it was packed, for it is only the ordinary two-car diesel: we expected to see a hauled train of six or eight coaches at this time of year! The passengers for the Grimsby direction wait to board while the crowd for Skegness surges over the bridge: it is a good job the local train is a double set!

While the passengers crowd on to the Skegness train the opportunity is taken to open the gates to get rid of the road traffic, and then there is a word on the phone with Thorpe Culvert to ask him to switch in to shorten the block section; there are a number of excursions to come and the first one which should have gone round twenty minutes ago looks as if it will arrive just in time to conflict with the delayed local train.

No sooner is the phone hung up that the South offers that tardy trip round the curve - 1X28 from Belper. It is offered to Wainfleet at once and the signals cleared (11, 12, 10). Although the local train will be ready to leave by the time the trip arrives the latter is sent first as it does not call at intermediate stations.

TRAIN ON LINE is signalled to Burgh as the down train at last leaves, and OUT OF SECTION signalled to the South. The relief, and the down train, are reported to Control, and the down inner home put up.

"We've got a rush on now", observes Mr. Moore: in fact he's been steadily on the go since the down relief turned up, and will be for the next hour or so. The Skegness local, anxious to leave, hoots loudly; "too late", says the signalman as 1X28 is almost here! The down train has cleared track H on its way to Burgh, and so the down starter (18) is put up. Then, half an hour late, TRAIN ON LINE is received from the South for 1X28, and TRAIN ON LINE passed on to Wainfleet. As the train is seen to enter track F the distant (10) is put up; while it negotiates the curve the gates are closed and when track F clears the curve down home (11) is put up.

Now OUT OF SECTION is received from Burgh for the down train. As we watch 1X28 finally clear track G the East starter (12) is put up, the bay platform starter (14) cleared and the very full Skegness train at last leaves the platform: the passengers will certainly be pleased to arrive at the seaside! OUT OF SECTION is signalled to the South for 1X28, and No. 14 put up. The South promptly offers the next train round the curve, the 8-20 SX Derby Friargate to Skegness, but it is refused. The East single line home (13) is cleared for the local train to draw forward to the starter, and as he clears track C that signal is put up.

A sigh of relief is breathed as Thorpe switches in, and promptly signals OUT OF SECTION for 1X28, so the local train is offered, the starter pulled off and TRAIN ON LINE signalled. At last, a quarter of an hour late, the train is on its way to Skegness, and No. 12 is put up as soon as he clears track G (fig 131).

The train from Derby can now be accepted from the South, and he signals TRAIN ON LINE at once! Because of the lateness of 1X28 this train is twelve minutes late going round, and while he creeps round the curve the delay to the local train is reported to Control. No. 11 is cleared to let the Derby train draw up to the starter. Before long Thorpe signals OUT OF SECTION for the Skegness local, so the Derby is offered and accepted. The starter (12) is pulled off (fig 132), TRAIN ON LINE signalled to Thorpe, and as the train clears track F No 11 is put up. We do not report trains round the curve to Control: they are the responsibility of the South.

Now the South offers train 1E87, the 9-20 SX Nottingham Victoria to Mablethorpe; it is accepted and offered on to Burgh at once. The gates are still

130 The 9-20 SX peak summer train from Nottingham to Mablethorpe bowling merrily over Firsby level crossing on Wednesday 31 July 1963. The engine is 61172. As well as showing the erstwhile 3-arm signal, this picture is a good illustration of the overlapping gates in the middle of the level crossing.

131 The local train which should have left for Skegness at 11-15 was delayed by the late running of the down train, and did not leave till 11-27, see text. So excursion 1X28 from Belper, also very late, has been sent ahead: it is still in section to Wainfleet, causing the local to wait at the East down starter. But Thorpe has just opened to shorten the block section, and has accepted the local. The signal has been pulled off and ON LINE signalled to Thorpe, the Thorpe non-pegger under the diagram shows TRAIN ON LINE. Mr. Moore is at No 12 lever looking up the line to the South where, hard on the heels of 1X28, the 8-20 ex Derby Friargate due at 11-22, is waiting. It is now 11-28, and as soon as the local train clears track G No. 12 can be restored and the Derby train accepted. The two cut down levers, Nos. 7 & 8, will be noted: these control the motors and are cut short as a reminder to the signalman not to give them a big heave as they merely operate electrical contactors. The two large dials above the block shelf indicate the state and correct operation of the motors. Towards the right of the picture is lever No. 24, one of the North bolt locks: it, too, is cut short as the bolt locks have been changed from mechanical to electrical operation.

132 The waiting 8-20 from Derby has now been accepted from the South and is coming round the curve past the East: tracks F, E, & G are occupied on the diagram and the 'branch' pegger block instrument from the South is at TRAIN ON LINE. The Skegness local train has reached Thorpe, and he has accepted the Derby train, as shown by the Thorpe non-pegger instrument beneath the diagram at LINE CLEAR. So the East starter No. 12 may be pulled off, and the picture shows Mr. Moore as he completes the pull and the catch handle drops home: the clock shows 11-34 so the effects of crowding on the down local train have cost the Derby train seven minutes.

closed since the Skegness train left, so the down main signals (16, 17, 18, 15) are cleared and the handgates locked.

The Derby train is pulling away towards Thorpe, and as it clears track G No. 12 is put up and OUT OF SECTION is signalled to the South, who then signals TRAIN ON LINE on the down line for the Mablethorpe train, it is passed on to Burgh straightaway; the distant (10) is put up, and with the whistle shrieking B1 61092 bowls past with the train - he, too, is ten minutes late. The main gates are opened, OUT OF SECTION signalled to the South, the inner home (17) put up, and finally the train is reported to Control.

There is at last a pause for breath, but only just, for the South offers train 1Z22, an excursion via Lincoln for Skegness due round at 11-43, so we are now just about back to schedule. 1E87 having cleared track H, No. 18, the starter, is put up. Then we receive OUT OF SECTION from Thorpe for the Derby train, so 1Z22 is offered and accepted. The signals round the curve (11, 12, 10) are cleared. A brief interval, then Burgh rings OUT OF SECTION for 1E87; then after a short interval the South rings TRAIN ON LINE for 1Z22; TRAIN ON LINE is passed on to Thorpe straightaway.

Traffic grumbles its way over the crossing, and the opportunity is taken to phone the North with information of the traffic for him off the mid-day pick up goods. The distant (10) is put up as 1Z22 rounds the curve, and as soon as it clears the junction at the South he offers us excursion 1X31 from Leicester for Mablethorpe. It is offered on to Burgh, the gates closed, and the down main signals cleared. By this time 1Z22 is on its way to Thorpe, and so the East signals 11 and 12 are put up and OUT OF SECTION signalled to the South. There are now a few minutes respite while 1Z22 reaches Thorpe and we receive OUT OF SECTION. Then we receive TRAIN ON LINE from the South for the Mablethorpe. TRAIN ON LINE is signalled to Burgh and the handgates locked. The train runs past in charge of a small Brush diesel (now known as class 31), the signals put up, the handgates unlocked and the main gates opened. OUT OF SECTION is signalled to the South.

Thorpe now offers the returning Skegness local train due at Firsby at 12-2, which means he has left Wainfleet; the Mablethorpe train is reported to control, and the South offers round the curve train 1X32 from Rugby for Skegness. It is offered on straightaway to Thorpe and the signals pulled off (11, 12, 10), in the hope that as it has left Little Steeping it will get round before the local train from Skegness arrives. A minute or so later Burgh signals OUT OF SECTION for the Leicester-Mablethorpe train, and before long Thorpe rings TRAIN ON LINE for the Skegness local. It is doing well, bearing in mind how late it was leaving on its last journey. There must have been some smart station work all along the branch, and it seems now that it will probably arrive at the East as the Rugby train goes round. We watch its progress on the track diagram and sure enough just as it enters track A the Rugby train turns up and the South signals TRAIN ON LINE, which is passed on to Thorpe straightaway. The local train will be checked a little, but as the main line connection is not due till 12-11 there should be no problem. We watch the Rugby make its way round the curve, restoring the signals as it clears the track circuits. Once track E is clear the motors are reversed and No. 5 signal cleared for the local train. OUT OF SECTION is signalled to the South for 1X32. The gates are closed, the handgates locked, No. 6 signal cleared, and three rings given on the platform bell tell the staff that the train is arriving. By now 1X32 has reached Thorpe and we receive OUT OF SECTION from him and we signal to him OUT OF SECTION for the local train. Nos. 5 & 6 signals are put up and the motors restored. There being no sign of the up train from Grimsby, the gates are opened to release the road traffic.

Then Burgh offers the up train, which means that it has left Willoughby. While we wait the control phone selector is heard stepping - the call is for us and it rings. It appears that there is trouble with the down pick up goods due shortly. There is a further wait and then Burgh signals TRAIN ON LINE. The train is offered to the South, the gates closed and the up main signals cleared (35, 38, 39, 40). Four rings on the platform bell announce its impending arrival: a six-coach train hauled by Brush type 4 diesel D1569, instead of the usual two-car unit. The distant (40) and home (39) are put up.

The Skegness local train, due out at 12-18, is offered to Thorpe and the signals (14, 13, 12) cleared for him to depart. The up train is quite busy and overstays its platform allowance: it is nearly five minutes late away. TRAIN ON LINE is signalled to the South, and as it draws away OUT OF SECTION is signalled to Burgh. The inner home (38) is put up, the Skegness train leaves and TRAIN ON LINE is signalled to Thorpe.

Now Burgh offers the mid-day up through goods which we accept. The Skegness train disappears round to the East, Nos.14 & 13 are put up, and the gates opened. Hardly is this done, than the South offers the down pick up goods, and signals OUT OF SECTION for the up passenger. The up starter, No. 35, is put up. A report is made to Control; then track G is observed cleared by the departing Skegness train so No. 12 is put up. Two or three minutes later Thorpe signals it OUT OF SECTION. A few more minutes elapse before the South signals the pick up goods TRAIN ON LINE. The gates are closed. In the middle of the second wind the South block bell calls but it must wait until the gates are shut, and before that is completed Burgh signals the up through goods TRAIN ON LINE, so this is answered first. Then the call from the South is answered and he rings '7 bells', i.e. 'Stop and Examine'; he follows up with a phone call telling us that a wagon on the pick up goods has a 'hot box' - which confirms the earlier report of trouble. Yet another delay: the defective wagon will have to be removed from the train and we have the up goods on its way and a following through goods on the down line right behind the pick up. It is agreed that the defective wagon will be detached at the North after the up goods has gone through as there are wagons to be collected anyway. The home and inner home (16 & 17) are cleared for the pick up to pass through the station. The approaching up goods is offered to the South and the up line signals (35, 38, 39) cleared; we wait for the indicator to show that the South distant is clear and then we can clear our distant, No. 40. TRAIN ON LINE is signalled to the South as the train rattles through, the signals restored and OUT OF SECTION signalled to Burgh. As B1 61179 chugs slowly forward with the pick up the North is called on the phone to tell him that the pick up will have to cross over to allow the following goods to pass. The home signal is put up as the goods passes, one wagon with smoke pouring from the overheated axlebox. The South signals OUT OF SECTION for the up goods. The handgates are released and as the pick up goods reaches the North the inner home is put up and OUT OF SECTION signalled to the South, who promptly offers the following through goods, but we

133 Five days prior to the sequence described in the text we see a B1 approaching the station on the 12-15 down goods. Running along merrily - no hot box to cause delay that day!

accept this up to the home signal only at '13 bells' (3-5-5, i.e. section clear but overlap blocked). Then 2-4 (block back inside home signal) is signalled to Burgh as the up line will be obstructed by the ailing pick up.

There are four rings on the bell from the North asking for the release of the crossovers, and so bolt lock 48 is reversed. As always there is road traffic waiting so the gates are opened. In the distance along the line to the south we see the through goods getting nearer, and after what seems an agonisingly long wait, but is in reality about 2 or 3 minutes, just as we decide that the gates had better be closed, all at once the South signals TRAIN ON LINE and the North rings 'down line clear', so bolt lock 48 is restored and the gates hastily closed. The goods is offered on to Burgh; the signals (16, 17, 18) are cleared (he is already past the distant), and he gives a blow on the whistle as he puts steam on. The handgates are locked, and TRAIN ON LINE signalled to Burgh. The train slogs past, steadily picking up speed, and as he gets clear of the station Nos. 16 & 17 are put up, OUT OF SECTION signalled to the South, and the gates opened once more. Watching the diagram, as soon as track H is clear No. 18 is put up. Now the bolt locks are reversed to release the North frame. Before the next main line trains are due he has an hour to safely stow the defective wagon and deal with the traffic to be deposited and collected. There is one more trip to go round the curve in about ten minutes' time, but then the Station Box can take a breather after a long spell of continuous activity, and so this is a convenient point at which to close this sequence.

This chapter has recalled Firsby's traffic patterns, and recounted some trains of events; perhaps, also, something of its importance as a junction has been shown. A variety of operations has been outlined: express and local passenger trains, goods trains and excursion traffic; the work of the station staff; the effects of late running and overcrowding; and the constant attention and anticipation required to deal expeditiously and safely with out of course and conflicting movements.

CHAPTER 10

AVE ET VALE

There was a story I heard in childhood of a traveller who arrived at a small spick-and-span rural station. The one member of staff was smart in his uniform busily tidying up, and the traveller exclaimed "Why all this fuss? This isn't Kings Cross you know!" The reply was instant and emphatic - "Mebbe it aint, but we're the same Company!" And Firsby was part of the same company that operated the world's longest non-stop run, ran the famous streamlined trains, and finally the world's fastest steam engine. Away from the main lines there was less glamour, but the secondary and rural lines provided a valuable service much missed to-day. How fortunate I am to have spent my early life at Firsby during some of the good years of railways. Many regard the period before 1914 as their hey-day, but after grouping the railways - not least the LNER - achieved in their main services standards of excellence surpassing anything earlier, and never attained since, and some of that excellence and devotion to duty filtered down to the less exalted parts of the system, even though some of the rolling stock was getting rather old.

Then the aim was to run a complete goods and passenger railway: none of to-day's fragmentation, or inane labels like inter city, network something or other, or - worst of all - that alien and quite inappropriate epithet metro. And in those days, too, the train was still the quickest, most comfortable, and civilised way to travel (not to mention the safest, which it still is). Moreover traffic was carried far and wide along that network of secondary and branch lines in which country junctions such as Firsby played an important part. Recounting to me a 1960s mix-up which left passengers stranded, a Firsby railwayman was emphatic: "Now in Fred Easter's day before the war that wouldn't have been allowed to happen". Yes, those were the days, and I am certain that I am not alone in wishing that Firsby junction, along with many others and their rural railway network were with us still. Salute, then, to Firsby, and to the staff who spent their working lives there in the public service.

So now it is farewell, a long farewell, to all the greatness; gone are the Station, the South, the East, the North. All that is left is the curve built to avoid Firsby: now it does so with a vengeance, leaving Firsby off the beaten track once more. Perhaps, who knows, among the ruins of the station the cries of *Firsby, Firsby, change for Skegness and Spilsby,* and many others, may still echo down the tunnels of time to haunt future occupants of the station houses. My final anecdote recalls a concert in Firsby Hut (fig 48), which I clearly remember though I would have been only about 10 years old then. The occasion was a visit by a concert party from Louth, who travelled by train of course. One of their number was a gentleman who performed songs at the piano; he was a composer and lyricist, and during the afternoon before the show he wrote and composed a song for Firsby, which of course he performed at the concert, probably its only performance ever! The verses are forgotten, but the chorus of that song still rings in my ears:-

Firsby O Firsby, the station it is grand.
If you want to go to Spilsby or to Skeggy by the sea
The porter says "Get out of it and have a cup of tea!"
Firsby O Firsby, it's on the G N line.
They clip your little ticket till there's nothing of it left
At Firsby, rain or shine.

How could I forget it? Passengers waiting for connections may have had other opinions, but in many ways Firsby station was grand, and to the youngster that was me it will ever be so. Let that be our final tribute.

134 (above) The winter snows of early 1947: the snow clearing team at the Skegness bay platform about 3-30 pm on a Sunday afternoon in February. The engine with the plough is a rare visitor to Firsby, ex-GER veteran J15 No. 5439 built in 1899; behind it is a Gresley V2, another type not seen on the East Lincolnshire line except for a brief spell on the expresses early in the war, while in the rear is an ex-GNR engine, probably an 0-6-0. This was the first weekend since the start of the snow that I was able to get home from Skegness, and even then it was by railway bus to Burgh and thence train to Firsby. The snow clearing team were working on the Skegness branch that weekend, and were able to clear one track, so I returned to Skegness on the Monday by train.

135 (opposite, upper) The GER J15 taking water on the Sunday afternoon when the Skegness branch was cleared, the enginemen taking an interest in photographer's antics. Of interest is the rear view of the old name-board at the end of the up platform, showing its construction. (Its front is shown in fig 17).

136 (opposite, lower) One of the never ending jobs that had to be done - cleaning the carriages of the Skegness local train. Mr. Dickson in action, vigorous action it would seem by the amount of movement of the brush during the fraction of a second the camera shutter was open! Middle to late March 1947, for there are still vestiges of snow about.

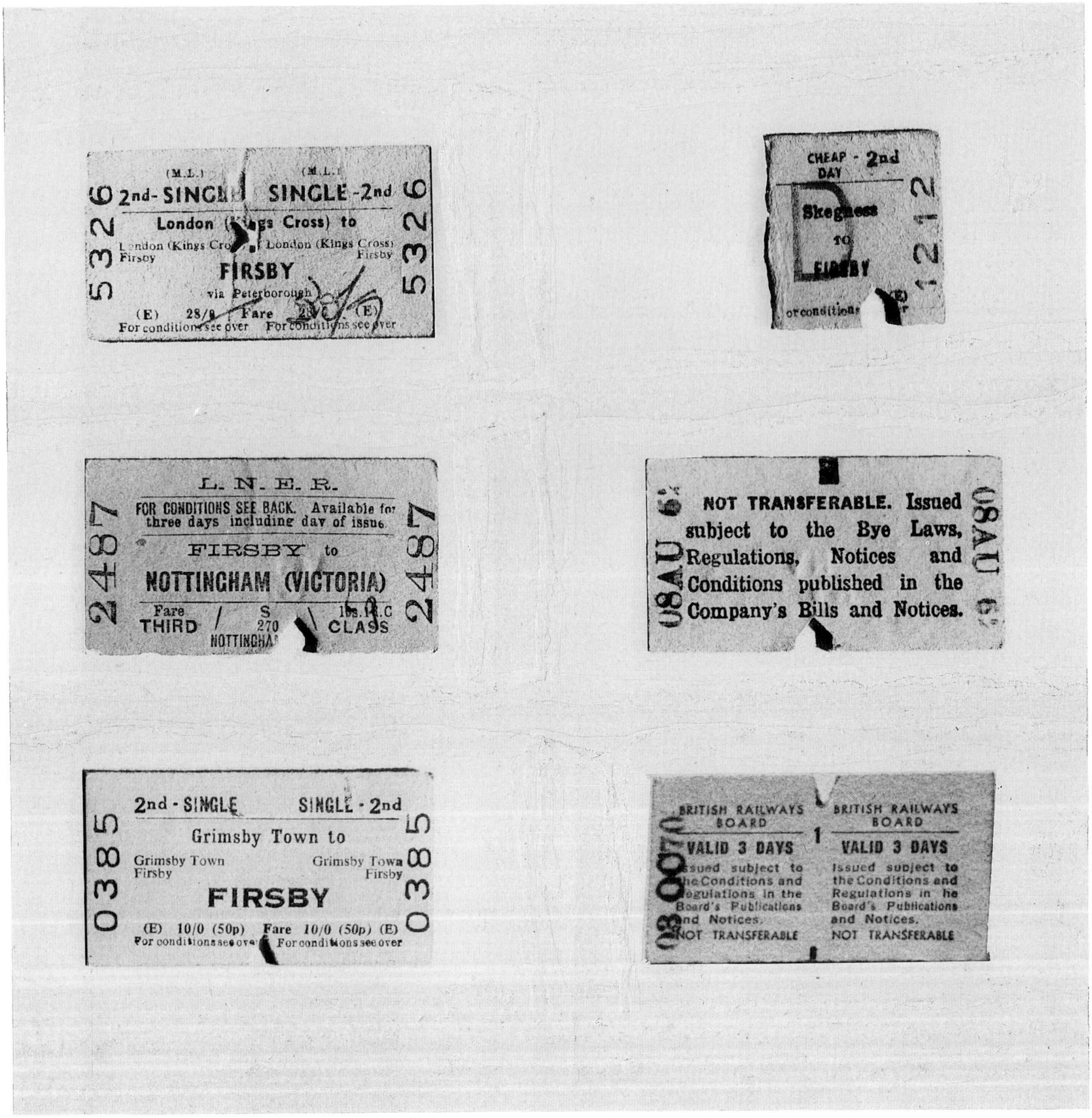

137 Some tickets to and from Firsby. Those in the two upper rows were used by the author. Of interest is the LNER ticket from Firsby to Nottingham issued 15 years after nationalization. The Kings Cross ticket is 'via Peterborough': before intermediate stations were closed such tickets were 'via Peakirk'. The Grimsby to Firsby ticket was used by Mr. Clayton (fig 39) on 3 October 1970, the last weekday of service.

BIBLIOGRAPHY

The following books are of direct interest to Firsby -

The Spilsby & Firsby Railway, A. J. Ludlam, Locomotion Papers No. 154, Oakwood, 1985.

Firsby to Wainfleet & Skegness, S. Walker, KMS, Boston, 1987.

The Lost Railways of Lincolnshire, S. E. Squires, Castlemead, 1988.

The East Lincolnshire Railway, A. J. Ludlam, Oakwood Library of Railway History, Oakwood, 1992

Railways of Lincolnshire, P. Anderson, Irwell, 1992.

References to Firsby, sometimes only in passing, appear in a number of works covering GNR & LNER history and operations, for example -

The Louth, Mablethorpe & Willoughby Loop, A. J. Ludlam, Locomotion Papers No. 162, Oakwood, 1987.

The New Line, S. Walker, KMS, Boston, 1985.

History of the Great Northern Railway, Charles Grinling, (revised Borley & Hamilton Ellis), Allen & Unwin, 1966.

The Great Northern Railway, O. S. Nock, Ian Allan, 1958. (This work includes at p. 100 the origin of the somersault signal.)

The Great Northern Railway, (3 vols), J. Wrottesley, Batsford, 1979.

Some Branch Lines in East Lincolnshire, M. F. Barbey, *Railway Magazine,* May 1958, p. 316.

Two Routes to Skegness, S. C. Jenkins, *Railway Magazine,* July 1985, p. 308.

POSTSCRIPT

This book goes to press at the end of the first season of successful steam excursions to Skegness, and there is talk of more in the future. So, contrary to expectations, Firsby once more resounds to the sound of a steam engine pulling away with a trip from the East and the South. Long may it continue.